Translation in Global News

Translation in Global News examines how news agencies, arguably the most powerful organizations in the field of global news, have developed historically and how they conceive of and employ translation in a global setting.

Incorporating the results of extensive fieldwork in major global news organizations such as Reuters, Agence France-Presse and Inter Press Service, this book addresses the new pressures facing translation as the need for a flow of accurate information which must transfer successfully across geographic, linguistic and cultural boundaries becomes increasingly more important.

Bringing together the common concerns of globalization studies, media studies, sociology and translation studies, *Translation in Global News* is the first text of its kind to deal extensively with the issue of translation in the context of global news and will be key reading for students of translation studies, media studies and journalism, as well as anyone with an interest in how news is transferred around the world.

Esperança Bielsa is Lecturer at the Department of Sociology at the University of Leicester. She is the author of *The Latin American Urban Crónica: Between Literature and Mass Culture* (2006) and co-editor of *Globalization, Political Violence and Translation* (2008).

Susan Bassnett is Professor in the Centre for Translation and Comparative Cultural Studies at the University of Warwick. She has previously published over twenty books including *The Translator as Writer* (co-edited, 2006), *Translation Studies* (third edition, Routledge, 2002) and *Postcolonial Translation: Theory and Practice* (co-edited) (Routledge, 1999).

Translation in Global News

Esperança Bielsa and Susan Bassnett

Routledge
Taylor & Francis Group

LONDON AND NEW YORK

First published 2009
by Routledge
2 Park Square, Milton Park, Abingdon, OX14 4RN

Simultaneously published in the USA and Canada
by Routledge
270 Madison Ave, New York, NY 10016

Routledge is an imprint of the Taylor & Francis Group, an informa business

© 2009 Esperança Bielsa and Susan Bassnett

Typeset in Times New Roman by
Taylor & Francis Books
Printed and bound in Great Britain by
TJ International, Padstow, Cornwall

British Library Cataloguing in Publication Data
A catalogue record for this book is available from the British Library

Library of Congress Cataloging in Publication Data
Bielsa, Esperança.
Translation in global news / by Esperança Bielsa and Susan Bassnett.
   p. cm.
Includes bibliographical references.
1. Journalism–Translating. I. Bassnett, Susan. II. Title.
PN4784.T72B54 2008
418'.02–dc22

                                                                2008012572

ISBN 10: 0-415-40973-X (hbk)
ISBN 10: 0-415-40972-1 (pbk)

ISBN 13: 978-0-415-40973-5 (hbk)
ISBN 13: 978-0-415-40972-8 (pbk)

Contents

Acknowledgements

This book has been made possible by the generosity of the Arts and Humanities Research Council, which provided the funding for a research project that included a series of seminars that brought together academics, graduate students and practitioners in the field of news translation. We are particularly grateful to Professor Yves Gambier of the University of Turku and to Professor Christina Schäffner of the University of Aston who acted as advisors to the project throughout its period of existence.

We also wish to thank Mario Lubetkin and Miren Gutiérrez of Inter Press Service, Eric Wishart of Agence France-Presse and Anthony Williams of Reuters, as well as all the journalists from Inter Press Service and Agence France Presse's offices in Montevideo and Reuters headquarters in London, who generously welcomed us in their organizations and participated in interviews.

Thanks are also due to colleagues and postgraduates in the Centre for Translation and Comparative Cultural Studies and the Centre for the Study of Globalisation and Regionalisation at the University of Warwick, in particular Red Chan, Chris Hughes, Alberto Orengo, Jan Aart Scholte, Joy Sisley and Claire Tsai. We are also very grateful for secretarial assistance to Janet Bailey, Caroline Parker and Maureen Tustin.

An earlier version of Chapter 2 appeared in *Language and Intercultural Communication* (Vol. 5: 2, 2005). A version of Chapter 3 has been published in *Global Networks* (Vol. 8: 3, 2008). Chapter 4 is based on 'Translation in Global News Agencies', published in *Target* (Vol. 19: 1, 2007), with kind permission by John Benjamins Publishing Company, Amsterdam/ Philadelphia, www.benjamins.com.

The appendix was published electronically on the University of Warwick website following the symposium in April 2004.

Introduction

This book derives from research in two distinct interdisciplinary fields: translation studies and globalization studies. Both have expanded enormously in the twenty-first century, in an age when intercultural communication is becoming increasingly significant, but have developed along parallel tracks, with researchers in each area often quite unaware of how closely their work may be connected. As is shown in Chapter 1, translation studies has tended to focus on debates about the nature of linguistic equivalence, the problems of untranslatability and the complex relationship between language and culture, while globalization research has, perhaps surprisingly, tended to disregard language issues even while it has expanded research into other aspects of global communication and interchange. Part of the explanation lies, of course, in the linguistic beginnings of the one and the sociological beginnings of the other, but as both fields have expanded and have at times used the same theoretical apparatus in their analyses, such as the work of Benedict Anderson, so the points of contact have increased and it is therefore timely to bring diverse research strands together in a discussion of a field that has major implications both for globalization and translation: the international transmission of news.

This book considers the ways in which news agencies, arguably the most powerful organizations in the field of global news, have developed historically and how they conceive of and employ translation in a global setting. At the same time, it explores the highly complex set of processes that underpin the interlingual transfer of news items, processes that raise important questions about the boundaries and indeed definition of translation itself.

For while the accepted notion of translation is that it is a linguistic act that involves the transfer of material from one language into another, what emerges when we start to look at the ways in which the news is translated shows us that translation is very much more than this.

When journalists talk about 'translation', they tend to be thinking of what others might term 'literal translation', and, as will be shown, some of the views expressed by people who prefer to call themselves 'international journalists' rather than translators reveal that the way in which they conceive of translation is very different from the way in which linguists or language teachers might. Information that passes between cultures through news agencies is not only 'translated' in the interlingual sense, it is reshaped, edited, synthesized and transformed for the consumption of a new set of readers. It would seem that in the global media world, the very definition of translation is challenged and the boundaries of what we might term translation have been recast.

Through an investigation into the mechanics of news translation, this book seeks to establish a basis on which further research into global communication strategies can evolve. Globalization studies, media studies, sociology and translation studies have vast areas of common interest, yet have not until recently started to share those common concerns. The question of global information flows is linked to the ways in which the media constructs news stories, and the transfer of those stories often involves moving not only across space but also across language and cultural boundaries.

Globalization, as is argued in Chapter 2, makes our world appear smaller and more homogeneous. The idea of global flows and the World Wide Web are images of interconnectedness that suggest that local spaces are decreasing in importance. The dominance of English as a global information language has added to this view, and there is evidence of the decline and disappearance of some local languages, a trend directly linked to the ideological domination of certain world languages. But there is another story beyond these assumptions: even as we acknowledge global communication networks as vital to world economic development, there are signs of a revival of local interests, most notably through the proliferation of new nationalisms and regional conflict zones. The current situation in Africa, the unresolved conflict in the Balkans, the Middle East, Afghanistan are all examples of localization struggles in which global and local forces are inextricably bound together.

At such a time, understanding local differences is of crucial importance, and here the role of translation is central. Western politicians who rushed into Afghanistan announcing that henceforth democracy would prevail and all Afghan women would be released from the burka forthwith completely failed to grasp how Afghan culture functioned and what weight traditional social patterns would continue to carry. Indeed, it is questionable whether a Western concept of democracy is exportable at all, since history would suggest the opposite. After the assassination of Benazir Bhutto in Pakistan in January 2008 and her legacy of party leadership to her 19-year-old son and unpopular husband, the Western media was surprisingly silent on the desirability of political dynasties, probably because it is a concept that does not sit comfortably with Western democracy and yet cannot, in the Pakistani context, be easily explained away or dismissed.

This book looks at global communication through an examination of translation practices, both diachronically, through an account of the globalization of news in the nineteenth and twentieth centuries, and synchronically, in terms of contemporary journalistic practice. It is hoped that anyone with an interest in how the news is transferred around the world will find something of interest here. It is also hoped that this study may serve as a starting point for further research into media and internet translation, a rich and relatively unexplored field that is already posing all kinds of challenges for translators. Above all, it is hoped that these preliminary findings will encourage more interdisciplinary work and will encourage both students and practitioners working in media studies, translation studies and sociology to share information and ideas.

1   Power, language and translation

Translation in the twenty-first century

The emergence of translation studies as a distinctive field of research has had considerable impact across a number of disciplines since its early tentative beginnings in the late 1970s. Opinion is divided as to whether or not translation studies can be classified as a discipline in its own right, and the term 'interdiscipline' is probably the most favoured term at present (Snell-Hornby et al., 1994). But regardless of debates about the name and nature of the subject area, what is clear is that discussion of translation has grown steadily in importance since then and has become significant in a wide variety of fields, from literary studies to post-colonial studies, from socio-linguistics to discourse theory, from business studies to international relations and globalization studies. Understanding something of what happens when translation takes place has come to be seen as necessary and important.

Translation as a metaphor for intercultural exchange serves also as a key image for the start of the twenty-first century, a century that is already one of massive movement of peoples around the planet on an unprecedented scale. Millions of people are displaced, some by wars and repressive governments, others by failed harvests, famine and economic catastrophe of one kind and another. Millions have left their homelands, abandoning their culture and language and seeking to start a new life in another place. In such circumstances, there is a heightened awareness of cultural difference and a greater need to reach out across cultural and linguistic boundaries than there has ever been before. This is reflected increasingly in literature, and many of the great writers of our age have changed languages, crossed borders and experimented with the unfamiliar: writers such as Vladmir Nabokov, Josef Brodsky, Milan Kundera, Samuel Beckett and Carlos Fuentes, and literary theorists such as Julia Kristeva and Tsvetan Todorov follow on from James Joyce, Joseph Conrad and Franz Kafka, and find themselves anew by translating themselves through the use of other languages. The pain of exile can result in extraordinary creativity, and is also a means of writing differently, because exiles, like translators view their world from more than one perspective.

When the history of the twenty-first century is written, attention will be drawn to the great rift that opened up between the Christian and Islamic worlds, resulting in the destruction of the Twin Towers in New York on September 11, 2001, the war in Iraq and the renewal of savage fighting in Afghanistan. Time and again commentators in the media have raised questions about misunderstanding between peoples, about misinterpretation, in short, about mistranslation. In the immediate aftermath of 9/11 a call went out to universities and translation bureaus across the United States trying to track down anyone who might have some knowledge of some of the languages used in Afghanistan and the surrounding areas. Since the start of the conflict, hundreds of young soldiers have died, uncounted numbers of civilians and many translators and interpreters.

At times of conflict, the role of the translator who produces either written or verbal versions of what is said in another language becomes foregrounded and deeply ambiguous. The task of a translator is to render what is said or written in one language into another, but where there is a highly charged situation that task is extremely difficult. Reliance on the competence of a translator involves trust, trust that he or she will adequately render the message originating elsewhere. Both parties, speaker and hearer, are dependent on the skills and good faith of the translator, and nowhere more so than in a war zone.

In the Middle Ages, when heralds brought news from the battlefield back to the prince controlling the conflict, there were occasions when they were punished by mutilation or even death for being the bearers of unwanted news. Some translators have suffered similar fates, and international organizations such as Reporters Without Borders regularly update the list of journalists, including translators and support staff, killed and imprisoned in trouble spots around the world. Bearing messages from the other side is fraught with danger and often translators risk their lives for the job they do. Some sixty Iraqi interpreters working for the British in Iraq have been murdered since the start of the conflict, and in August 2007 *The Times* ran a front-page story on the plight of ninety-one Iraqi interpreters and their families who, the story claimed, have been abandoned by the British government, in contrast with the special arrangements made by Denmark to protect its interpreters, with asylum as an option.

The ambiguities of translation

The role of the translator has been, and still is, burdened with suspicion and anxiety, for it is the translator who brings across the unfamiliar, who mediates between cultures that may well be violently antagonistic to one another and perhaps have a long history of misunderstanding between them. Translating therefore requires very special skills that go far beyond the linguistic. Just understanding what words might mean in the abstract is not enough; the translator needs to grasp what the words can signify in each particular context and then has to try and render those additional layers of meaning. Not for nothing has it been said that the primary task of the translator is to translate not what is there but what is *not* there, to translate the implicit and the assumed, the blank spaces between words. The difficulty of doing this effectively is immense.

The history of the discovery of the Americas by Europeans and sub-sequent establishment of colonial settlements is also a history of translation. Interestingly, key figures in the mythologizing of early colonialism were women: Pocahontas in the north, La Malinche in the south. La Malinche in particular has aroused strong views: on the one hand, she is seen as a vital instrument in the establishment of a relationship between the Spanish under Cortés and the native American population; on the other hand, she is seen as a traitor, as a betrayer of her own people, a woman whose linguistic fluency assisted a process of colonialization and enslavement. La Malinche in many respects symbolizes the ambiguous position of the translator, a figure who mediates between worlds, whose loyalties are to both the originator of the message and its destinee. The verdict on La Malinche remains two-sided: she can be seen as a heroine or as a betrayer, just as an armed guerrilla can be seen as a freedom fighter by one group and as a terrorist by another.

The role of the translator similarly can be seen from a dual perspective: on the one hand, the translator makes communication between cultures possi-ble, enables people with no access to the language of another people to open up a dialogue. On the other hand, the translator may collude in a process that either establishes or reinforces an unequal power relationship between peoples. Post-colonial scholars such as Tejaswini Niranjana and Vicente Rafael have highlighted ways in which translation was used as an instrument of oppression, either by reducing native culture to an accessible object or by inscribing and reinforcing the colonizers' perspective of that culture (Niranjana, 1992; Rafael, 1988). Though, ideally, translation can open up a new channel of communication between cultures, it can also reinforce the status quo and effectively restrict the import of new ideas, new literary forms and anything that contradicts the established perception of the target lan-guage audience.

It is, of course, a fact that not all languages and cultures have, or are perceived as having, equal power and status. The very terminology of 'min-ority' languages, for example, already implies an inequality. Some languages have assumed greater significance than others, through political, economic and even geographical factors. The history of colonialism is an extreme example of unequal power relations between languages, but languages have held greater or lesser status for centuries. Latin was the high-status language of Europe until the late Renaissance, for example, when gradually vernacular languages rose in prestige and came to acquire even greater cultural capital from the eighteenth century onwards. It should always be remembered, therefore, that an act of translation is not a process that takes place on a horizontal axis, but rather on a vertical axis, with one language, either the source or target, in a superior position to the other. Inevitably, this affects how translation takes place because the strategies employed by the translator will vary.

The basic activity of translation involves a translator taking a text, either written or oral, and changing it into another language. In doing this, there are all kinds of constraints, most obvious of which is the linguistic. Put at its simplest, no two languages are ever sufficiently alike for the identical structures and vocabulary to be used to express the same thing. Geographical proximity, relationships between languages, close links between societies do not ensure identical linguistic structures. Edward Sapir's statement about linguistic difference is as valid today as it was when he first wrote it in 1956: 'No two languages are ever sufficiently similar to be considered as representing the same social reality. The worlds in which different societies live are distinct worlds, not merely the same world with different labels attached' (Sapir, 1956: 69).

This means, of course, that a translator has to work within the constraints of the two languages, which may be considerably different from one another. Take, for example, politeness conventions operating in a northern European language and in Japanese. Forms of address vary enormously according to criteria of social status, age, gender and familiarity, and to make a mistake could cause embarrassment at best, offence at worst. Or consider the vast difference in rhetorical conventions between French public speaking and English, where the former draws upon a sophisticated set of discursive norms, while the latter taps into a vein of irony and possibly also a powerful vein of religious allusion that can be traced back to the seventeenth century.

Summarizing the complex operation that is translation in their book on translation and power relations, Maria Tymoczko and Edwin Gentzler write:

> Translation thus is not simply an act of faithful reproduction but, rather, a deliberate and conscious act of selection, assemblage, structuration, and fabrication – and even, in some cases, of falsification, refusal of information, counterfeiting, and the creation of secret codes. In these ways translators, as much as creative writers and politicians, participate in the powerful acts that create knowledge and shape culture.
>
> (Tymoczko and Gentzler, 2002: xxi)

Translation therefore involves negotiation, it involves conscious selection and it involves re-creation in the target language. Tymoczko and Gentzler also suggest that there are times when translation may also involve more sinister forms of textual manipulation that they term falsification and refusal of information. What they mean is that a translator can add to a text or, perhaps a more frequent act, leave out parts of it. Translators can, and often do, expand a text with explicatory details, or delete those parts which are deemed too unfamiliar and inaccessible to a target audience. The strategy of omission, which is extremely common, effectively prevents target readers from ever having full access to the source. Tymoczko and Gentzler see this as almost a form of censorship, and indeed research into the history of translation of repressive regimes such as fascist Italy or Spain in the 1930s does indeed show that omission was a deliberate strategy directly linked to centralized censorship. However, it is important to note that omission is a key strategy in the translation of news items, where material is tailored to the needs of a specific local audience. As will be discussed later in this book, the translation of news items can involve all kinds of textual manipulation, including synthesis, omission, explication and a host of other textual strategies.

Early translation studies research in the 1970s wrestled not so much with manipulation, but with the problem of defining and determining equivalence. Could a translation be said to be equivalent to the source text in every way, and if not, why not? Eugene Nida explored the problem by establishing a distinction between what he called formal and dynamic equivalence, a binary distinction that can be traced back to the Romans and the categorization of translation as either word-for-word or sense-for-sense. Hence formal or word-for-word translation adheres more closely to the structures of the source, while dynamic or sense-for-sense translation abandons formal equivalence for a more broad-ranging view, and rejects any notion of equivalence as sameness.

In the 1980s Katharina Reiss and Hans Vermeer developed their *skopos* theory, which postulated that the objective of the target text would determine how it was translated. This meant that a translation could deviate enormously from the source and yet fulfil the original purpose. Vermeer's theories have therefore been extensively used in discussion of technical translation and reception and are particularly helpful for any discussion of news translation. Underpinning *skopos* theory is the idea of equivalent effect, rather than of any binary equivalence on the linguistic level. Hence the translation of an instruction manual, for example, should adhere to the norms and conventions appropriate to the target audience, rather than following the codes of the source text, which may lead to a wide divergence in semantic, syntactical and even broader cultural terms and, as a result, obscure meaning. We have all seen menus or hotel instructions or similar texts that have been translated literally, with no regard for the conventions of the target readers and so appear absurd. Equivalent effect is probably the best one can hope for with most translations, when we reflect that what happens in translation is that a text is read, decoded and then reshaped in the target language to accommodate differences of structure, style, context and audience expectation.

The cultural turn

As translation studies began to develop out of linguistics and literary criticism, questions of power relations began to play an increasingly significant role. The so-called cultural turn in translation studies back in the early 1990s ensured that translation would henceforth be seen not as an isolated activity, taking place in a kind of vacuum, but as an act directly linked to the world in which translators work. The cultural turn stressed the need to take into account the circumstances in which translation occurs, broadening the object of study from the purely textual and taking into account both source and target contexts. Itamar Even-Zohar elaborated a cultural model based on a study of translation history that showed how translation varied at different moments: a culture actively seeking to renew itself, even one that perceived itself in the grip of nationalistic fervour, would translate more texts than a culture which saw itself as culturally self-sufficient (Even-Zohar, 1990). So, for example, during the nineteenth century in the period of revolutionary ferment as countries across Europe demanded independence from the Ottoman or Austro-Hungarian empires there was a huge surge of translating activity which fed into the emerging new national literary movements. At the same time, as Britain and the United States consolidated their global economic power, so translation activity slowed down and became, as it is today, marginal and not necessary either to the state or to literature. The present translation boom in China, however, offers an example of a nation in a period of radical change and expansion, importing as much as it can from elsewhere.

Even-Zohar's cultural hypothesis was followed by research that looked more closely at the strategies used by translators themselves. Lawrence Venuti elaborated a dichotomy originally formulated by the German Romantic scholar Friedrich Schleiermacher in 1813, who suggested that translators are faced with the choice of either taking the reader back to the text or bringing that text across to the readers (Schleiermacher in Schulte and Biguenet, 1992). When the first option is followed, features of the source text and its context are reproduced with the result that the final product might seem strange and unfamiliar, and this process has come to be known as *foreignization*. This form of translation deliberately foregrounds the cultural other, so that the translated text can never be presumed to have originated in the target language. In contrast, when a text is adapted to suit the norms of the target culture, this is known as *domestication*, since signs of its original foreignness are erased. Venuti prefers the term *acculturation* rather than domestication, and draws attention to the ideological implications of transforming the foreign into something that has lost all sense of its foreignness, which he sees as problematic, since by erasing traces of the foreign, the translator prioritizes the needs and expectations of the target culture over the source. Venuti argues that this practice has been at the heart of imperialist translating strategies and proposes what he calls 'dissident' translation practice, in which the foreign is deliberately not erased, so as to compel target readers to acknowledge the otherness of the source: 'Foreignizing translation is a dissident cultural practice, maintaining a refusal of the dominant... [it] enacts an ethnocentric appropriation of the foreign text by enlisting it in a domestic cultural political agenda, like dissidence' (Venuti, 1992: 148).

Venuti's proposal, though it may seem at first glance to be extreme, raises an important question. He suggests that a translation practice which deliberately foregrounds the foreignness of a text could cause readers to rethink their own domestic norms and conventions, and recognize that by erasing the unfamiliar what is happening is actually a form of ethnocentric textual violence. The act of retaining the foreign therefore challenges the status quo and becomes a form of protest against the hegemony of domestic literary practices. This, Venuti suggests, is 'abusive fidelity', a translation technique that aspires to a faithfulness that is not dependent on fluency.

Of course this debate also raises the question of the status of translations and of translators. Translation, especially in the English-speaking world, is a poorly paid activity, often regarded as marginal and of less significance than other forms of writing. The skills required to be able to translate tend to be seen as less valuable and less 'creative' than other writerly skills. Venuti takes issue with this view, and deliberately entitled his book *The Translator's Invisibility*, pointing out that the vital role played by a translator has tended to be ignored, to be invisible. His solution to this is for translators to become more visible, to develop innovative translation practices that will remind readers that the text they are reading did not originate in the language in which they are reading it, and to demand equal recognition as authors of works that they have translated.

Translating and the news

Making translators more visible is a laudable aim and one that clearly resonates in the literary world. However, when we consider news translation, the translator's visibility is a completely different matter, and Venuti's foreignization hypothesis ceases to hold any value. In news translation, the dominant strategy is absolute domestication, as material is shaped in order to be consumed by the target audience, so has to be tailored to suit their needs and expectations. Debates about formal and stylistic equivalence that have featured so prominently in literary translation cease to matter in a mode of translation that is primarily concerned with the transmission of information, though ideological shifts remain fundamentally important in all types of translation, as will be discussed more fully later.

Research into the strategies of news translation is still relatively underdeveloped, but already there is interest worldwide in examining the processes of exchange and transfer in the media. For in addition to the international news agencies, global TV channels now transmit news bulletins to millions of people and there is an expectation that news will be broadcast day and night, with regular updates throughout a twenty-four-hour period. The phrase 'breaking news' has entered everyday language, and news channels use this to heighten expectations and create a sense of anticipation. Regular updates with breaking news are now essential in an age of blogs and internet chat-rooms. If we take the situation of news reporting in Iraq and Afghanistan, for example, though the journalists embedded with the troops file their stories at speed, they may still be pre-empted by bloggers who go directly online with their version of events and bypass intermediary organizations such as agencies, translators or journalistic and television bureaus. Speed in transmitting information is vitally important in a highly competitive new market.

Christina Schäffner is an expert in translation and discourse analysis, specializing in the analysis of political discourse. She draws attention to the absence of research into the phenomenon of translation in political text analysis, pointing out that it is through translation that information is made available across linguistic borders and that frequently reactions in one country to statements made in another country 'are actually reactions to the information as it was provided in translation' (Schäffner, 2004: 120). Stressing the importance of understanding this, she poses a series of questions about how translators are trained, how they select material, which particular ideological constraints affect translation and what causal conditions seem to give rise to certain types of translation. In short, she highlights gaps in our knowledge about the translation of political discourse, gaps that are just as wide in our understanding of the translation of global news. Research in translation studies into issues of language and power has mainly been applied to discussions of literary texts, but clearly such issues are fundamentally important in the analysis of other discourses also, particularly in the translation of news. What research in this field is starting to show is that translation is one element in a complex set of processes whereby information is transposed from one language into another and then edited, rewritten, shaped and repackaged in a new context, to such a degree that any clear distinction between source and target ceases to be meaningful. This is in total contrast to more established research into translation practice, particularly in the field of literary translation, where discussion is always in some way focussed around the idea of the binary distinction between source and target texts. Research into news translation poses questions about the very existence of a source and hence challenges established definitions of translation itself.

Moulding news material

The shaping of any news story is undertaken subject to a series of constraints which are both spatial and temporal. The newsworthiness of a story will be determined by its timing, by the circumstances within which the story has emerged. There may be editorial decisions to publish precipitately, or to hold back while circumstances change slightly. There will be decisions about the availability and/or desirability of photographic images. Those decisions will be made in-house, and will be affected by the ideological position of the newspaper and by the context in which that newspaper is produced. Spatial constraints will include word length, position on a given page and location of that page in the newspaper as a whole. A story about an earthquake that kills hundreds of people in one of the remoter parts of the world may be relegated to inside pages or only given a few lines, but if, for example, the earthquake happens in a region that is deemed to be more newsworthy, perhaps because it is a well-known holiday destination for readers or in a state where there are particular political sensitivities, it may be front-page news and be given wide coverage regardless of the final death-toll. The assembly of a newspaper follows the same pattern as that identified by Tymoczko and Gentzler for translation: it is a deliberate and conscious act of selection, involving the structuring, assembling and fabricating of information into a format that will satisfy the expectations of readers.

Part of that process may well involve handling stories that have originated in another language. In some cases, newspapers will publish features that have appeared in print in other parts of the world, and this form of translation will involve some of the same strategies as we encounter in other forms of translation. It is, however, worth noting that direct translation of a text written in one language into another is probably the least common form of news translation; far more common is the restructuring of material in a form congenial to the target readership.

In the case of direct translation of a published text, though there may be a relatively straightforward transmission of content, there may have to be a series of adjustments in terms of stylistic conventions. So, for example, the British use of pithy, often outrageously comic headlines that is such a feature of the tabloid press will have no equivalent in those cultures where the headline is often a full sentence supplying information on the article that follows. The British tabloid press go in for comic headlines, such as the infamous *Sun* headline during Anglo-French trade wars which read 'Hop off you frogs', or the appalling 'Gotcha!' during the Falklands war which reported the sinking of the *Belgrano* in 1982. This would be unacceptable practice in many countries, though unacceptable to British readers would be the use of hyperbole and highly florid rhetoric that is the norm in much of the Arabic world, for example. Translating such rhetoric literally has the effect of making the speaker ridiculous, as has been the case with the English translations of extracts from speeches by political figures such as Colonel Gaddafi or Saddam Hussein.

The acceptability of shifts of register also varies considerably between languages. In Arabic or Farsi, for example, register shift is relatively unproblematic, but in English it is highly significant. The inappropriate use of a single word in a text can have an adverse effect on its reception, given that in English consistency of tone and style are seen as desirable. In English, shifts of register can signal major shifts of meaning or of position, which is not the case in languages where such shifts are not significant.

Another British tendency is the use of direct speech in articles, to give an impression of immediacy and authenticity. This is a convention that would be unpopular were it to be translated without amendment into German, for example, where direct speech is not generally acceptable in higher-status newspapers. Then there is the question of different ways of developing a story. In some cultures, the narrative of a story follows the pattern of starting at the beginning, then moving through the development of that narrative to a conclusion, through a process of gradual exposition. The effect for the reader is one of slowly discovering more details until the final exposition at the conclusion of the article. Elsewhere, in other systems, such as the British, the full story may be given in the first paragraph and the rest of the article is then an elaboration of the opening statements, with no surprise at the finale.

In their useful book *The Translator as Communicator*, Basil Hatim and Ian Mason devote a chapter to the problems of translating texts that present a particular form of argument. They distinguish between 'through-argumentation', which they define as the statement of a thesis and its subsequent substantiation, and 'counter-argumentation', which they define as 'citing an opponent's thesis, rebutting this and substantiating the point of the rebuttal' (Hatim and Mason, 1997: 127). In their discussion of these two processes, the authors use examples taken from English and Arabic and show how very different conventions and reader expectations can apply in different contexts. Research indicates a strong tendency towards counter-argumentation in English, while the opposite holds in Arabic, where the preference is for through-argumentation. So, for example, the English penchant for starting an article with a statement that is then rebutted through extended counter-argument would not be understood by readers who expect a line of argument to take a sequential, step-by-step explicatory form. From even this limited range of examples, it is clear that a translator working with texts that have already been published has therefore to make adjustments in terms of stylistic conventions to accommodate the very different expectations of a new set of readers. What is also clear is that although superficially this situation might appear to be due to those different stylistic conventions, there are strong ideological implications. Hatim and Mason state simply that text type constantly functions as 'a carrier of ideological meaning' (Hatim and Mason, 1997: 142). Recognizing this is an important step in developing greater understanding of the processes of news translation. The norms operating in different cultures will determine how a story is presented, and in consequence there are bound to be ideological implications when we compare the different ways in which the same story is told. In Chapter 7, we shall examine differences between the British, French and Italian press coverage of the trial of Saddam Hussein, where the employment of different journalistic norms and readers' expectations result in subtle distinctions in the presentation of well-documented material.

Reshaping material

Where the picture becomes more complex, however, is where there is no published written text that is to be translated for republication. Instead, there may be a mass of material assembled in different ways and from different sources. Speaking at a symposium organized at the University of Warwick in April 2004, Eric Wishart, the then editor-in-chief of the Agence France-Presse, distinguished various stages of translation in what he termed the news-gathering procedure, citing as an example an explosion on a train in North Korea that had happened days before. The first news came through to the Agence France-Presse from the Chinese News Agency, in Chinese and also in English. (The Chinese account gave the death toll at 3,000.) There was nothing from the North Korean News Agency, but stories then came from South Korean agencies, in Korean and in English. Translators in local bureaus worked on putting the Chinese and Korean versions into English, after which the texts were sent to a central editing desk. A French writer in Hong Kong was translating the English into French:

> So you've already got two steps: you've got the original story in Korean on Korean news agencies, written in English, in the bureau, translated by a Korean journalist who speaks English, stories translated to the central editing desk in Hong Kong by a French writer, because there was no French writer in the Seoul bureau who translated the story into French. And it's real time, big time. Reuters are on the case, AP are on the case. You've got to get the news out fast.
>
> (Wishart, unpublished transcript, 2004)

Wishart then pointed out that once the story is sent round the world, it is translated again into other languages for local use. All this happens at high speed, with the spectre of competition for first place always looming large. A story may therefore have gone through several different translations before it reaches its destination, being reshaped at every stage in accordance with linguistic and stylistic constraints.

An additional stage is added when interviews are part of the news story. In such a case, there may be an interpreter who 'translates' for the journalist, who then files a story based on that exchange. Here the journalist is entirely dependent on the skills of the interpreter, but in writing up the interview there will necessarily be an editing process. Indeed, editing is a crucial part of all news translation. Unlike literary translation, where the size and shape of the original are usually preserved, in news translation there has to be editing that will involve synthesizing and cutting. As Wishart pointed out, there are millions of words moving around the world every day in a constant state of being translated. Reuters, for example, works with some eighteen languages, with a daily output equivalent in volume terms to the Bible, of which approximately 60 per cent is in English, with Japanese coming second with 7 per cent. These staggering figures serve to emphasize the difficulty of establishing any clear understanding of what is actually involved in news translation.

What we can say with some assurance is that as material is moved across language boundaries, so it also undergoes all kinds of other transformations, which may include cutting, editing, synthesizing several different sources, or reworking a piece that purports to be a 'literal translation'. What is also clear is that there is considerable uneasiness on the part of many journalists to define themselves as translators, preferring to call themselves journalist-translators, international reporters or, more commonly, simply journalists with knowledge of another language. Such definitions emphasize the target culture, focussing on the rewriting aspect of the translation process, where cultural understanding and knowledge of the target norms are seen as more crucial than the actual stage of interlingual transferral. For many journalists, a translator is seen as someone who provides a literal version of a text that would not be suitable for publication. The journalist then reworks that text into one that can be utilized. Needless to say, this is a view contested by professional translators who object to seeing their work downgraded in such a way. This divergence of perspectives is examined at greater length in Chapter 4 and 5.

In addition to problems that involve the ability to decode cultural knowledge, there is also the fundamental question of translating extremely long texts. A series of interviews might run to a hundred thousand words, and it would be time-consuming and pointless to translate such texts in their entirety. What has to happen, then, is a process that involves selection and synthesis: the one thousand words might end up reduced to several hundred, so the task involves not only interlingual transfer but an ability to reduce and edit for the target audience. Here again the general view is that this is the task of the journalist.

In her article based on her experiences as a news translator for Formosa Television (FTV), Claire Tsai describes the stages of her daily work, from being handed an assignment to seeing it broadcast. She makes a distinction between the work involved as a translator for a visual medium and that of a translator working with print, noting in particular time constraints and the requirement for there to be usable footage, but nevertheless, the points she makes about the freedom of the translator can serve for both types of translation. Asking the question about the freedom of the translator ('just how free is "free"?') she states that: 'TV news translators are given the freedom to restructure and reorganise messages under the one condition that the target texts should always be congruent with the source texts in meanings, nuances and facts' (Tsai, 2005: 149). But she goes on to add that often there are drastic cuts and major restructuring of the material, particularly when the translator is given more than one source or is dealing with very densely packaged material. She also points out that from her experience, exercising this kind of freedom involves considerable effort.

The task of creating this kind of text is not, as Reuters' journalist Anthony Williams (2004) argues, 'translation pure and simple', though translation studies scholars would, of course, note here that there is no such thing as translation pure and simple, for all translation involves the manipulation of an original as it is reshaped for a new audience. However, it remains a fact that the very word 'translation' carries with it a particular history, where debates about the responsibility of the translator to be 'faithful' to the original have been going on for centuries. What the study of news translation adds to the debate is in endeavouring to define quite what an original text might be. An original may be thousands of words of text that have to be cut down to a minimum, or it may be a string of loosely connected interviews and versions that have been derived from different sources, and those sources may well have originated in entirely different linguistic and cultural contexts. There is no clear sense of what an original is when we are looking at news translation, and in such circumstances the old idea of translation being an act that takes place across a binary line between source and target can no longer be upheld.

Indeed, in many respects news translation is more similar to interpreting than to translation, if we take translation to mean the rendering of a text written in one language into another. The interpreter like the news translator works in real time, has to synthesize material very rapidly and may not have a clearly definable single source. An interpreter may also be operating within and across several languages. So, for example, if a conference is being held in English at which many of the speakers have diverse language backgrounds and the event is being interpreted into a language in which none of them are competent, this could be seen as a parallel to the case outlined earlier where a journalist has to make sense of something that has gone through several languages, being reshaped each time. However we look at it, what is going on is not a straight binary transfer.

One of the foremost interpreting scholars, Daniel Gile, has sought to understand the different research developments in translation studies and interpreting studies. He notes that the two have different histories, with research in translation being much older and more focussed on ideological, cultural and sociological issues, while the more recent research into inter-preting has been very process-oriented. He also notes that there is a gap between practitioners in both fields and researchers, just as there is a gap between journalists and researchers in news translation. Gile calls for greater collaboration between translation and interpreting research, arguing that the two can contribute to greater understanding of both fields of activity, given that epistemological and methodological problems are not dissimilar. One way of bringing these two areas together could well be through further investigation into news and media translation.

One major link between news translation and interpreting is the require-ment of both to domesticate the foreign for a target audience. Just as an interpreter will reshape material in such a way as to ensure maximum clarity for an audience, regardless of the structures of the original, so too will a journalist tailor material for a specific set of readers. Here there is a clear distinction between the way in which research into translation studies has been moving and research in its embryonic form into news translation. Domestication or acculturation as a translation strategy has been hotly debated and has, in recent years as mentioned above, tended to be seen as undesirable by many translation studies scholars, because it is deemed to be, in ideological terms, a practice that appropriates the other. Yet such appropriation is essential in interpreting and in news translation, where the objective is to bring a message to the target audience in a clear, concise and totally comprehensible way.

Research into news translation has tended to fall between other fields of investigation that have received much more attention. On the whole, research in translation studies has focussed on other text types and has tended to ignore news translation. Research in media studies and journalism has focussed on single language cases, and has paid scant attention to inter-lingual transactions. In this book, we have endeavoured to bring together research in these distinct, yet ultimately inter-related fields on the grounds that it is timely and necessary to bring an interdisciplinary approach to the study of news translation. For the transmission of news around the globe is happening every minute of every day and is increasing in importance with advances in technology that ensure ever greater speed of communication. It is therefore important for us to have more understanding of what happens between the occurrence of an incident somewhere in the world and the time when we hear about it locally. We already have a great deal of helpful research into the ways in which news comes to be published or broadcast in particular contexts, and we have a growing body of research that looks at processes of translation. What we need to do now is to put together those diverse strands of research in order to move towards a greater understanding and awareness of how intercultural news material is created and transposed.

2   Globalization and translation

Two fundamental features of globalization are the substantial overcoming of spatial barriers and the centrality of knowledge and information, resulting in the increased mobility of people and objects and a heightened contact between different linguistic communities. Thus, globality is manifested not only in the creation of supraterritorial spaces for finance and banking, commodity production (transnational corporations and transworld production chains) and global markets, but also in the increased significance of travel and international movements of people (mass tourism, business travel, migration and exile), and the consolidation of a global communications system which distributes images and texts to virtually any place in the world. These developments signal, in spite of the predominance of English as a global lingua franca, an exponential growth in the significance of translation, which becomes a key mediator of global communication. Yet language and translation have been systematically neglected in the current literature on globalization. This chapter introduces central theoretical perspectives on globalization and translation. It critically examines current theories of globalization and interrogates their lack of attention towards translation. It also formulates an attempt to understand the significance of translation in a global context, conceptualizing its analytical place in globalization theory and its key role in the articulation of the global and the local.

Globalization is generally associated with the shrinking of our world and the possibility of instant communication across the globe. Widespread metaphors of accelerated mobility, such as those of flows and of the information superhighway, only serve to emphasize this, creating an image of the world as a network of highly interconnected places in which space ceases to be significant. The present focus of globalization theory on mobility and deterritorialization has obscured the complexities involved in overcoming cultural and linguistic barriers, and made the role of translation in global communications invisible. In this chapter, our first task in approaching current theories of globalization is thus to interrogate their lack of attention towards translation as a key process in the development of global connectedness. We will then argue that translation is central for an understanding of the material conditions that make possible global connectedness and that a focus on translation has important consequences for the way that globalization is understood today.

Globalization has been defined as 'the widening, deepening and speeding up of worldwide interconnectedness in all aspects of contemporary social life' (Held et al., 1999: 2) and is notably not a new phenomenon, but was already present in the world religions and empires of antiquity. Moreover, globalizing tendencies are inherent in the development of capitalism, which functions through its geographical expansion, and the nineteenth century was a major period for the development of global connections. While some theorists point to the deep historical roots of globalization and maintain that 'different processes of globalization have developed at different times, followed different trajectories and tempos' (Held et al., 1999: 26), it can be argued that the origins of contemporary globalization are to be found in the early modern period, when Europe's political and military expansion took place.

What is new about the present phase of globalization, which Roland Robertson designates as the 'uncertainty phase', starting in the late 1960s, is the intensification of global interconnectedness and the heightening of global consciousness (1992). This is generally related to several key developments. The first is the new extreme mobility of capital, associated with the deregulation of financial markets and new information technologies which dramatically enhanced the communication capabilities of firms (Castells, 2000: 96). Second, David Harvey (2000) emphasizes the fall in the cost and time needed to move commodities and people, and the overcoming of space as a crucial factor. The movement of people involves not only both highly skilled and unskilled labour, but also holiday travel, which has become widespread after the fall in price of train and car travel first, and later of the jet plane (Lash and Urry, 1994). Third, Robertson points to a sharp acceleration in the means of global communications and the consolidation of a global media system. Manuel Castells speaks of a communication revolution led by television since the 1960s, while in the 1980s and 1990s two factors contributed to radically transform the global television market. The first of these is the development of satellite communications, which would make possible instantaneous and simultaneous transmission around the globe 24/7. The second development refers to the global expansion of ownership of television sets which, as Held et al. remark, did not become generalized outside the West until the 1980s and 1990s (Held et al., 1999: 357). Today, through the use of fibre optic cable and satellite technology, it is possible to communicate instantly and cheaply with virtually any place and to follow significant world events from our television screens with images and commentary in real time.

These developments have led to the constitution of supraterritorial social relations and to the overcoming of spatial boundaries, either virtually in cyberspace or materially through instant communications technology. This supraterritorial dimension, which refers to the substantial transcendence of territorial geography in social relations, is what distinguishes, following Jan

Aart Scholte, contemporary globality from earlier periods of globalization in which transplanetary connections between people were already widespread (2005: 61). Thus, transworld simultaneity and instantaneity are new features which express that social relations now take place substantially beyond territorial space, and distinct from an earlier longer-term trend towards a shrinking world through the development of transportation technology, which still took place within territorial geography (2005: 62).[1] In what follows, the main characteristics of globalization in relation to space and mobility will be sketched in more detail.

The compression of the world

A central feature of modernity, closely related to an understanding of globalization as the shrinking of the world, is what David Harvey approached in terms of time–space compression, by which he designated a speeding up of the pace of life while also overcoming spatial barriers (1989: 240). The notion of time–space compression implies a degree of interconnection and interdependence, which puts an end to the relatively isolated worlds of feudalism that were linked to territorial boundaries. Harvey shows how in the Renaissance a slow revolution in the conception of space and time took place from which scientific, objective notions of space and time emerged. These were incarnated in the improvement of maps and the invention of the chronometer, which were both based on notions of uniform, measurable space and time. The Enlightenment appropriated the Renaissance conceptions of time and space and gave them a new meaning in the context of its project for human emancipation, in which universality is not threatened by cultural diversity:

> Maps, stripped of all elements of fantasy and religious belief, as well as of any sign of the experiences involved in their production, had become abstract and strictly functional systems for the factual ordering of phenomena in space ... They also allowed the whole population of the earth, for the first time in human history, to be located within a single spatial frame ... The diversity of peoples could be appreciated and analysed in the secure knowledge that their 'place' in the spatial order was unambiguously known. In exactly the same way that Enlightenment thinkers believed that translation from one language to another was always possible without destroying the integrity of either language, so the totalizing vision of the map allowed strong senses of national, local, and personal identities to be constructed in the midst of geographical differences.
>
> (Harvey, 1989: 250)

Clock time and empty space are the structural conditions that make possible the representation of the world as homogeneous and uniform, free from the particularisms of place: 'The global map, in which there is no privileging of place (a universal projection), is the correlate symbol of the clock in the "emptying" of space' (Giddens, 1991b: 17). In the Enlightenment, both maps and translations expressed emerging interconnections conceived in terms of the relationships between well-defined identities linked to particular places, which for the first time could be visualized on a global scale. As we will see below, the dramatically increased mobility of recent decades will come to threaten this sense of fixed identity and the very distinctiveness of place.

During the second half of the nineteenth century the process of time–space compression was strongly accelerated with key technical innovations such as the telegraph, the widespread use of steam shipping and the expansion of the railway network, which led to increased spatial integration. In addition, as Harvey points out, the Enlightenment sense of progressive time was fundamentally questioned after 1848, and a new conception of 'explosive' time emerged while a new sense of relative space started to replace the certainty of absolute space (1989: 261). The increasing internationalization of the economy and the conquest of space were accompanied by a new sense of fragmentation that would determine the crisis of representation to which modernist art was a response.

Closely connected with time–space compression is what Anthony Giddens has conceptualized as the disembedding of social systems in modernity, which presupposes the uniformity of time measurement and time–space distantiation or the separation of time from space, which in pre-modern times were connected through place (1991a: 17–20).[2] Giddens defines disembedding as 'the "lifting out" of social relations from local contexts of interaction and their restructuring across indefinite spans of time–space' (1991a: 21) and points to 'symbolic tokens' such as the money form and 'expert systems' as the main types of disembedding mechanisms. Both money and expert systems bracket time and space so that social interaction is increasingly separated from the particularities of places or locales and comes to depend upon interactions with those who are absent in time–space. Money 'is a mode of deferral, providing the means of connecting credit and liability in circumstances where immediate exchange of products is impossible' (1991a: 24), while expert systems 'bracket time and space through deploying modes of technical knowledge which have validity independent of the practitioners and clients who make use of them.' (1991b: 18). Writing should also be viewed as an important disembedding mechanism, as it effectively makes communication possible across time and space.[3]

Bearing in mind his conception of time–space distantiation and of the disembedding of social systems in modernity, it is not difficult to see how, for Giddens, modernity is inherently globalizing (1991a: 63). Accordingly, he defines globalization as 'the intensification of worldwide social relations which link distant localities in such a way that local happenings are shaped by events occurring many miles away and vice versa' (1991a: 64). Globalization thus refers to a further intensification and 'stretching' of time–space distantiation, to the dynamics of presence and absence that disembedding mechanisms introduce by bracketing time and space.

The space of flows

During the present phase of globalization, which corresponds to a change in the capitalist mode of production in the past decades that has been conceptualized as post-Fordism, flexible or disorganized capitalism, an acceleration of the process of time–space compression has taken place. Scott Lash and John Urry have described this qualitative change as follows:

> The paradigmatic media of mobility during the epoch of organized capitalism were railroads, telephone via wire cable, postal services and later road networks. All of these brought 'time–space convergence' and 'time-cost convergence' mainly on a *national* scale (although their role in the British Empire should be noted). By contrast the paradigmatic mobility media of disorganized capitalism are fibre-optic cable, satellite communications and air transport. They have led to time–space and time–cost convergence on a *global* scale.
>
> (1994: 25)

Lash and Urry, and other theorists of cultural globalization such as Arjun Appadurai, have centred on the global circulation of material and non-material goods, conceived in terms of flows (of capital, people, commodities, information and images), pointing to its increased profusion and speed in the past decades. Thus, for Appadurai the 'mobile and unforeseeable relationship between mass-mediated events and migratory audiences defines the core of the link between globalization and the modern' (1996: 4). On the other hand, Lash and Urry refer to Giddens' conception of time–space distantiation, further stressing the consequences of the speeding up and stretching out in the circulation of flows: 'this acceleration, which simultaneously "distantiates" social relationships as it "compresses" time and space, is leading to an emptying out of both subjects and objects. This accelerated mobility causes objects to become disposable and to decline in significance, while social relationships are emptied of meaning' (1994: 31). Globalization and the increased speed of flows not only lead to the flattening of both objects and subjects, but also generate a new sense of time derived from electronic time, which Lash and Urry call instantaneous time. Instantaneous time takes place at a speed beyond the realms of human consciousness, brings a decline in significance of clock time and is the final stage in the abstraction of time.

The implications of such a conception of hypermobility and speed are maybe nowhere clearer than in this notion of instantaneous time, which can be taken to generate an accompanying loss of meaning in any realm of social life. Thus, for Lash and Urry, the instantaneous character of contemporary time facilitates its *use* by powerful organizations which often results in a flattening and a disembedding of social relations. But the use of instantaneous time can also be enabling for ordinary subjects. They can view and evaluate different cultures at the flick of a switch, or via high speed (or almost instantaneous) transport. This enables the rapid and extensive juxtaposition of, and comparison between, different cultures and places.

(1994: 243, original emphasis)

How can cultures be grasped, let alone evaluated, 'at the flick of a switch'? Can they be examined and compared without recourse to translation? While mobility, by necessity, generates the need for translation between different cultural and linguistic contexts, theories focussed on the global circulation of flows deny or minimize its very existence. One reason for this is that their emphasis on instant communication makes translation processes in global communication invisible, much in the same way as translation has been made invisible in literary critical commentary (Venuti, 1995) or in the experience of travel (Cronin, 2000). In all these cases, invisibility implies the assumption of transparency: that texts are unproblematically rendered in another language, just as the travel writer has unmediated access to a foreign reality. The nature of translation as a process which necessarily mediates between cultures is ignored.

This is related to another, more fundamental reason for obscuring the role of translation in global communication: the very focus of these theories on the circulation sphere,[4] which precludes any sustained analysis of translation (or, indeed, of any other productive infrastructure) as a material precondition for the global circulation of meaning. Global flows become in this way phantasmagoric and opaque to understanding, as Appadurai's insistence that they are 'complicated' and even 'mysterious' indicates (1996: 34–35). Thus, while this author does recognize and makes various references to the importance of the translation of concepts such as 'freedom', 'rights' and 'democracy' in different political and cultural contexts, he cannot provide an adequate explanation for the structural role of translation in cultural flows because of his very conception of the absolute primacy of the circulation sphere.

The predominant focus of theories such as Lash and Urry's or Appadurai's on the global circulation of goods and the consequent lack of analysis of the productive processes that shape and make current developments possible is avoided in the most elaborated conception of the space of flows: Manuel Castells' theory of the network society. For Castells, globalization is linked primarily to the revolution in information technologies of the 1970s, which became the motor for the expansion and rejuvenation of capitalism at the end of the twentieth century, just as the steam engine was the motor of the first industrial revolution. Informationalism, characterized by the fact that the main source of productivity is the action of knowledge upon knowledge itself (2000: 17), is thus for Castells the new material base of the socio-economic restructuring of the 1980s that gave rise to the network society.

Informationalism has 'spread throughout the globe with lightning speed in less than two decades, between the mid-1970s and the mid-1990s' (2000: 32). The informational economy is thus global. Castells defines a global economy, distinguishing it from a world economy, as 'an economy with the capacity to work as a unit in real time, or chosen time, on a planetary scale' (2000: 101), and points out that 'while capitalism is characterized by its relentless expansion, always trying to overcome limits of time and space, it was only in the late twentieth century that the world economy was able to become truly global on the basis of the new infrastructure provided by information and communication technologies' (2000: 101). The global economy which emerged in the 1990s is constituted by an informational core (financial markets, international trade, transnational production and specialized labour), but also by local or regional production disconnected from it, and is thus structured by asymmetry and inequality in its midst. Its basic unit is the network: the global production of goods and services is increasingly not performed by multinational corporations (which themselves have become decentralized internal networks) but by international production networks, composed of small and medium-sized firms in addition to multinational corporations (2000: 121–22).

Castells captures the new spatial organization of the informational society through the metaphor of the space of flows. The space of flows is characterized by the fluid mobility between those places that are connected to global networks and, at the same time, by spatial fragmentation and discontinuity: 'the switched-off areas are culturally and spatially discontinuous: they are in the American inner cities or in the French *banlieues*, as much as in the shanty towns of Africa or in the deprived rural areas of China or India' (2000: 33). The fragmentation of the space of flows finds its expression in the new industrial space, characterized by the technological ability to separate the production process in different locations, as well as in mega-cities, which are connected in a global network and increasingly less related to their regions.

Castells shares with Lash and Urry a belief in the 'gigantic leap forward in the reach and scope of the circulation sphere' (2000: 100) and points to the increasing autonomy of global financial flows from their economies, a result of the nature of informationalism. Thus, he asserts that 'money has become almost entirely independent from production, including the production of service, by escaping into the networks of higher-order electronic interactions barely understood by its managers' (2000: 505). In his conclusion to the first volume of *The Information Age*, he clearly identifies his basic underlying assumption that this epoch is marked by the autonomy of culture vis-à-vis the material basis of our existence, a vision which itself rests on the highly questionable distinction between a material, determining base and a determined superstructure, and does not take into account the fact that, as Raymond Williams has shown, culture is itself material production (1977).

In spite of this, Castells does not ignore the centrality of production. He dedicates extensive chapters to the transformation of work and of the capitalist enterprise, and even offers a detailed description of the social and intellectual context of Silicon valley, where the information technology revolution took place. His attention to the productive forces and the key role that Castells attributes to knowledge and information as the new material socio-economic base of the network society would seem to indicate that translation, as an important means for their global transmission, should occupy a significant place in his theories. Yet, it is completely absent from his account of the network society. This absence is all the more striking if one thinks that Castells is a Catalan, coming from a bilingual society in which language use is highly politically charged, who writes in English and has found, through a language that is not his own, a global audience. In addition, in his book he explicitly thanks his Russian wife for providing him with access to other languages. The reason for his silence on translation is thus not naivety about linguistic diversity or the politics of translation, but must be sought elsewhere. A clear indication in this respect can already be found in his prologue to *The Rise of the Network Society*, where he asserts that 'a new communication system, increasingly speaking a universal, digital language, is both integrating globally the production and distribution of words, sounds and images of our culture' (2000: 2). Castells does not see translation as an important process in the network society because he does not believe that linguistic diversity intervenes in its globalized core. In the distinction he makes between the spaces and times of capital and labour, a space of flows, of the instant time of computerized networks, and a space of places, of clock time of everyday life (2000: 506), the first is implicitly conceived as monolingual, while linguistic diversity, linked to place and not to the hypermobility of flows, is seen to belong to the realm of the second.

Castells' position in this respect is what Michael Cronin would characterize as neo-Babelian, and expresses a 'desire for mutual, instantaneous intelligibility between human beings speaking, writing and reading different languages' (Cronin, 2003: 59). Yet, in Castells' deterritorialized network society it is not English which becomes the global lingua franca, but the digital language of science and technology, a language not of countries but of multilocational, global networks. Thus, for Castells, the tools of informationalism are

> ... new telecommunication networks; new, powerful desktop computers; ubiquitous computing devices connected to powerful servers; new, adaptive, self-evolving software; new, mobile communication devices that extend on-line linkages to any space at any time; *new workers and managers, connected to each other around tasks and performance, able to speak the same language, the digital language.*
>
> (2000: 212, emphasis added)

This reduction of linguistic diversity is highly problematic. In the first place, as Cronin has shown, the neo-Babelian option does not make translation disappear, but merely transfers it to those who do not speak the dominant language, who must then doubly translate from and into the dominant tongue (2003: 60). Whether the conception of digital monoglossia implies a certain degree of technological determinism cannot be examined here. However, the fact that the digital language is not a naturally existing language linked to territory makes its translation, its relationship to other languages, very abstract and difficult to conceive. Second, Castells' neo-Babelianism cannot address actually existing translation practices that are a response to globalization. By focussing only on the language of technology, Castells chooses to ignore how linguistic diversity is dealt with at the very core of the network society, be it through processes of localization of technology or through the news stories that the media report worldwide, translated and in real time.

The analytical place of translation in globalization

David Harvey described the experience of postmodernity as follows:

> The whole world's cuisine is now assembled in one place in almost exactly the same way that the world's geographical complexity is nightly reduced to a series of images on a static television screen ... The general implication is that through the experience of everything from food, to culinary habits, music, television, entertainment, and cinema, it is now possible to experience the world's geography vicariously, as a simulacrum. The interweaving of simulacra in daily life brings together different worlds (of commodities) in the same space and time. But it does so in such a way as to conceal almost perfectly any trace of origin, of the labour processes that produced them, or of the social relations implicated in their production.
>
> (1989: 300)

Harvey is following here Marx's account of commodity fetishism according to which commodities acquire a ghost-like autonomy from their material or social relations of production. Globalization juxtaposes elements from distant cultures abstracted from the social contexts in which they have emerged, thus creating a fragmented and discontinuous experience. In this experience of simultaneity of the world's geography a key social relation that is obscured is translation, which necessarily mediates between different linguistic communities. Globalization theory which focusses primarily on mobility and flows is compelled to repeat this negation because its very focus on the circulation sphere prevents it from being able to deal appropriately with the social processes and relations of production that shape contemporary globalization.

A notable exception to this is Saskia Sassen's analysis of global cities. Sassen explicitly denounces the partiality of theories that emphasize the hypermobility of capital and information, the capacity for instantaneous transmission around the world rather than the infrastructure it presupposes (1998: 202). For her, 'introducing cities into an analysis of economic globalization allows us to reconceptualize processes of economic globalization as concrete economic complexes situated in specific places', thus recovering the 'localized processes through which globalization exists' (1998: xix, xx). Her account of global cities, by focussing on the social and economic processes that occur in the most fluidly connected points or nodes of the space of flows, solidly articulates the relationship between the global and the local in specific places, also breaking with views such as those of Manuel Castells and Zygmunt Bauman (1998) which emphasize the distinctive time–spaces of hypermobile capital and place-bounded labour. Thus, Sassen insists that:

A focus on the work behind command functions, on the actual production process in the finance and services complex, and on global market-*places* has the effect of incorporating the material facilities underlying globalization and the whole infrastructure of jobs typically not marked as belonging to the corporate sector of the economy. An economic configuration emerges that is very different from that suggested by the concept of information economy. We recover the material conditions, production sites, and placeboundedness that are also part of globalization and the information economy.

(1998: xxiii–xxiv, original emphasis)

Global cities constitute, according to Sassen, a worldwide grid of strategic places, a new geography of centrality that cuts across national borders and the traditional North–South divide (1998: xxv). Significantly, the global city, 'with its vast capacities for controlling hypermobile dematerialized financial instruments and its enormous concentrations of those material and human, mostly place-bound, resources that make such capacities possible' (2000: 218), contains dynamics of both mobility and fixity. It is this articulation of the spatialities of the global and the national that constitutes the global city into what Sassen calls an analytic borderland, a frontier zone which requires its own theorization and specification (2000: 220).

The conception of the global city as a frontier zone, a key place for the articulation of the global and the local, for the organization of the material infrastructures that make globalization possible, introduces an important theoretical move in globalization theory. If we have dedicated here some space to the discussion of what is primarily an account of economic globalization it is because we believe that Sassen provides a general framework within which it is possible to theorize basic processes, such as translation, that intervene in the material production of globalization. Moreover, we will maintain that translation, as a key infrastructure for global communication

(Held et al., 1999: 345),[5] can also be conceived as an analytic borderland where the global and the local are articulated, and is thus, in cultural globalization, the equivalent of global cities in economic globalization.

We mentioned above Raymond Williams' characterization of cultural practices as themselves material production. In this context, Lawrence Venuti has also argued that 'Translation exposes a fundamental idealism in philosophy by calling attention to the material conditions of concepts, their linguistic and discursive forms, the different meanings and functions they come to possess in different cultural situations' (1998: 106). This analysis will thus consider translation as a material precondition for the circulation of meaning on a global scale. Only by challenging its invisibility, which obscures the social conditions under which translation is performed as well as its role in mediating between cultures, will the mechanisms of cultural globalization be more fully understood.

Furthermore, if globalization is defined as increased connectivity (see the first, introductory section to this chapter), it is possible to identify a basic similarity between globalization and translation when we remind ourselves that 'translation is all about making connections, linking one culture and language to another, setting up the conditions for an open-ended exchange of goods, technologies and ideas' (Cronin, 2003: 41). An exploration of the processes of global connectivity on a concrete, material level is the fundamental contribution of translation to an understanding of the nature of globalization.

Globalization as translation

The asymmetries of globalization and the current inequalities in the production of knowledge and information are directly mirrored in translation, and this becomes visible when the directionality of global information flows starts to be questioned. Thus, some accounts of globalization have pointed to the number of book translations from English and into English as an indication of the power distribution in global information flows, where those at the core do the transmission and those at the periphery merely receive it (Janelle, 1991: 56–58; Lash and Urry, 1994: 28–29; Held et al., 1999: 345–46). The global dominance of English is expressed in the fact that, in 1981, books originally written in English accounted for 42 per cent of translations worldwide, compared with 13.5 per cent from Russian and 11.4 per cent from French (Janelle, 1991: 57). At the same time, British and American book production is characterized by a low number of translations: 2.4 per cent of books published in 1990 in Britain and 2.96 per cent in the United States (as compared with 9.9 per cent in France in 1985 and 25.4 per cent in 1989 in Italy) (Venuti, 1995: 12).

For Lawrence Venuti the dominance of Anglo-American culture is expressed not only in the low number of books that are translated into English, but also in the form in which they are translated according to the values of the target culture and thus following a domesticating strategy based upon fluidity and transparency (for an explanation of his conception of domesticating and foreignizing translation, see Chapter 1). Domesticating translations minimize cultural and linguistic difference under the appearance of transparency; they 'invisibly inscribe foreign texts with English language values and provide readers with the narcissistic experience of recognizing their own culture in a cultural other' (1995: 15).

More generally, transparency and invisibility also characterize the role of translation in globalization. It is therefore necessary to extend Venuti's analysis to elucidate what invisibility means on a global scale. First, the conception of instantaneous communication, of the unimpeded transmission of information flows, implies translation's invisibility and, at the same time, places new demands on translation. Thus, Cronin has noted how the information economy generates pressures on translation to become, on the one hand, a transparent medium of fluid interchange, and, on the other, to approximate more and more to the ideal of instantaneous transparency (2000: 111–12). The need for instantaneous communication in real time generates the need for simultaneous real-time translation, in which the human factor in translation is finally eliminated. Accordingly, Cronin notes the paradoxical nature of translation in the circulation of global information flows:

> The network underpinned by information technology brings Anglophone messages and images from all over the globe in minutes and seconds, leading to a reticular cosmopolitanism of near-instantaneity. This cosmopolitanism is partly generated by translators themselves who work to make information available in the dominant language of the market. However, what is devalued or ignored in the cyberhype of global communities is the effort, the difficulty and, above all else, the time required to establish and maintain linguistic (and by definition, cultural) connections.
>
> (2003: 49)

Global English dominance is expressed, on the one hand, in the sheer volume of English-language information in circulation. Thus, for example, current statistics on languages on the internet reveal the large number of English-speaking users (about one-third of the total), but also the even stronger predominance of English-language internet content (which is estimated at over half of the total).[6] On the other hand, translation, which makes it possible for people to have access to information in their own language, contributes to the global dominance of Anglo-American culture, as we have seen above for the case of book translations, which account for only the smallest part of the volume of translation, the bulk of which is in commercial translation, politics and administration and in the mass media.

Nevertheless, global or international English itself needs to be qualified and should be examined more carefully. Mary Snell-Hornby thus characterizes the global lingua franca: 'there is the free-floating lingua franca ("International English") that has largely lost track of its original cultural identity, its idioms, its hidden connotations, its grammatical subtleties, and has become a reduced standardized form of language for supra-cultural communication – the '"McLanguage" of our globalised "McWorld" or the "Eurospeak" of our multilingual continent' (2000: 17). International English, which in this sense can be viewed as a bad translation of itself, is a supraterritorial language that has lost its essential connection to a specific cultural context. It thus expresses in itself the fundamental abstractions derived from the disembedding or the lifting out of social relations from their local contexts of interaction.

Furthermore, there is an important political dimension linked to the global dominance of English that is emphasized by Pierre Bourdieu and Loïc Wacquant in their discussion of the 'new planetary vulgate' voiced by employers, international officials, high-ranking civil servants and media intellectuals. According to them, this Newspeak is the result of a new form of imperialism which universalises the particularisms of US society and universities under dehistoricized guises across the whole planet (2001: 2). The very use of the term 'globalization', 'whose upshot – if not function – is to dress up the effects of American imperialism in the trappings of cultural oecumenicism or economic fatalism and to make a transnational relation of economic power appear like a natural necessity' (2001: 4), is for Bourdieu and Wacquant an example of the way in which categories of thought derived from specific North American uses and interests are universally imposed. The consequences of what they see as a new cultural imperialism are pervasive and far-reaching: 'By imposing on the rest of the world categories of perception homologous to its social structures, the USA is refashioning the entire world in its image: the mental colonization that operates through the dissemination of these concepts can only lead to a sort of generalized and even spontaneous "Washington consensus", as one can readily observe in the sphere of economics, philanthropy or management training' (2001: 4).

However, the very fact that categories and concepts cannot be imposed directly but need to be translated or adapted to new cultural contexts identifies this view as one-sided and translation as a key process for the mediation between cultures. Before briefly describing the main forms that translation adopts in the global circulation of information it is thus worthwhile to recall Venuti's views on domesticating translation, his characterization of translation as a fundamentally ethnocentric act (1998: 10) and his emphasis on the violence that is exercised through it, which is echoed in his very definition of translation: 'Translation is the forcible replacement of the linguistic and cultural difference of the foreign text with a text that will be intelligible to the target-language reader' (1995: 18). This intelligibility implies a necessary degree of hybridization, through which a dominant discourse is effectively altered and rewritten in new terms. An account of globalization as translation needs to examine carefully the articulation of the global and the local as the dialectics between the dominance of English and translation as violence, between the imposition of the new planetary vulgate and domestication as an ethnocentric act of appropriation of the other.[7]

Globalization has caused an exponential increase of translation. The global dominance of English has been accompanied by a growing demand for translation, as people's own language continues to be the preferred language for access into informational goods. An area of significant growth in the translation industry in recent decades has been the activity of localization, through which global products are tailored to meet the needs of specific local markets (Cronin, 2003; Pym, 2004). In an informational economy characterized by instantaneous access to information worldwide, the objective of the localization industry becomes simultaneous availability in all the languages of the product's target markets. Translation values and strategies in localization and elocalization (website localization) are not uniform but combine elements of domestication and foreignization to market products that have to appeal to their target buyers but, at the same time, often retain exoticizing connections to the language of technological innovation (for an example, see Cronin, 2003: 16–17).

Similarly, translation plays a central role in negotiating cultural difference and in shaping the dialectics between homogeneity and diversity in the production of global news. We will discuss in the next chapter present trends towards the homogenization of global news. However, these need to be examined alongside domesticating translation strategies aimed at a fluid communication with target readers and exoticizing devices through which the discourse of the other is staged in the media (in, for example, English translations of Osama Bin Laden's tapes or Saddam Hussein's speeches). The next chapter explores the relationship between globalization and news, approaching the development of global journalism since the nineteenth century and the key role of the news agencies in historical perspective.

3 Globalization and news

The role of the news agencies in historical perspective

Globalization and the media

As we have seen in the previous chapter, the intensification of the consciousness of the world as a whole, the significant subjective dimension of globalization emphasized by Robertson, is related to the transformation of communications technologies and the consolidation of a global media system. The global media not only make instant and cheap communication possible across the world, they also promote an experience of global connectedness. In the past 150 years, electronic media, from the telegraph to fibre optic cable, satellite transmission and the internet, have made possible instant communication between distant places, thus contributing to what Anthony Giddens has approached in terms of time–space distantiation (see Chapter 2). On the other hand, communication technologies have shaped current processes of cultural globalization. We have seen how the experience of globalization is linked to the reduction of the world's geographical complexity to a series of images on our television screen, to the bringing together of different worlds in the same space and time. The role of the media in promoting images of simultaneity is pivotal in processes of cultural globalization and can be traced back to the first modern newspapers of mass circulation.

From the middle of the nineteenth century, the telegraph radically altered the way in which news was produced. The individual items of modern newspapers became no longer selected on the basis of spatial proximity but following newly emerging journalistic criteria of news relevance. This also implied that only the most recent events were newsworthy, and that increasing competition to break news started to take place. Giddens has emphasized the integration of printed and electronic media that took place since the telegraph started to be used for news transmission, and has pointed to two main features of the reorganization of time and space in globalizing modernity that the media – including both older media that still operate through the printed word like the newspapers and also newer media like television – both express and help to produce. The first is what he calls the collage effect that dominates the news: the media juxtapose stories and items which share nothing in common. While the time factor, both in terms of how recent events are and in terms of their consequential order, is all-important, the limitations that emanated from place have been virtually eliminated. The second feature of the mediated modern experience is the intrusion of distant events into everyday consciousness, an important expression of disembedding or the lifting out of social activity from localized contexts (Giddens, 1991b: 26–27). These features have led Giddens to assert that 'the media do not mirror realities, but in some part form them' (1991b: 27), thus highlighting once more the central role of the media in producing an experience of global simultaneity.

This idea can also to be found in Manuel Castells' conception of real virtuality. According to Castells, the end of the twentieth century has witnessed the integration of written, oral and audio-visual modalities of human communication through technological transformation and, most notably, the convergence in the second half of the 1990s of diversified and customized global mass media with computer-mediated interactive communication. This is not merely a qualitative technological change: in the past three decades, and led by television, there has been a communication explosion throughout the world through which we have come to interact 'endlessly and automatically' with the media (Castells, 2000: 362). In the past decade, this has culminated with the extension of the realm of electronic communication into the whole domain of life (2000: 394). As Benedict Anderson argued, newspapers made possible the existence of the imagined communities that would become the basis of the modern nation by establishing links between the members of a community who would never come to know each other face to face (1983). Today, virtual communities emerge around interactive communication through the internet, which thus generates new supraterritorial forms of bonding.

Castells' notions of the space of flows and of timeless time discussed in Chapter 2 are related to his idea of real virtuality, which is the product of the new integrated communication system based on digital, electronic technology. Castells more closely describes this as follows: 'It is a system in which reality itself (that is, people's material/symbolic existence) is entirely captured, fully immersed in a virtual image setting, in the world of make believe, in which appearances are not just on the screen through which experience is communicated, but they become the experience' (2000: 404). It is the emphasis on the integration of the diversity of historically transmitted systems of representation that is the key to understanding this notion of real virtuality, which is the outcome of the new system of communication's inclusiveness and comprehensiveness of all cultural expressions. Real and imaginary worlds communicate today in new and fluid ways, as people react to mass-mediated events giving them real impact while, at the same time, electronic communication takes over our whole lives.

The infrastructure for the production of global news was established during the second half of the nineteenth century, when the use of the telegraph became widespread and major news agencies for news gathering and distribution emerged and expanded their worldwide connections. From the 1840s, when the first telegraphic lines were set up, to 1858, when the first cable was laid across the Atlantic, and the following decade, when transatlantic communications became effective, the telegraph experienced, according to Marshall McLuhan, a fastest growth than any other technology, including the railroad (1964: 250). This new technology is linked to the constitution of global news agencies which, following Oliver Boyd-Barrett and Terhi Rantanen, were the first international media organizations and are among the first of the world's multinational corporations (1998: 1).

Global news agencies gather, process and transmit news to subscribing institutions around the world – they are news wholesalers, in Boyd-Barrett's terms. It is important to remember that news agencies are not only the global organizations with the biggest infrastructure for news gathering (typically present in over a hundred countries with permanent bureaus and with the technical means to send news teams fast virtually anywhere in the world), but also their very significant function in news processing and transmission, if their key but often invisible role in the global news market, which in many aspects echoes the invisibility of translation, is to be fully understood. News agencies produce raw information, but also more elaborate pieces of ready-to-print news reports, analysis and comment, which subscribing news organizations can freely reproduce, fully or in part, introducing any alterations or rewriting they consider necessary, without even acknowledging the source. It is also worthwhile remarking that news processing includes significant amounts of translation, which is fully integrated in the production of news. As we will analyse in detail in the next chapter, news agencies are effectively vast translating organizations with the technology and skills required for the production of fast and accurate translations, and offer a variety of linguistic products tailored to meet the needs of the biggest news markets and to facilitate global news circulation. On the other hand, since their creation, news agencies have had to strongly invest in technology so as to secure an ever faster news transmission. They have played a pioneering role in the use of new technologies such as the telegraph and information technology, which have significantly altered the very nature of news, and technological innovation continues to be a major area of competition between the news agencies.

The dynamics of globalization in articulating the local with the global can be examined in the way the news agencies operate. Global news agencies have important national connections, both in terms of their origins and in terms of regional areas of influence. As Boyd-Barrett and Rantanen remark, the agencies were vital components in the armoury of the nation state, and key in the dissemination of their 'national image' in global markets (1998: 5). Global news agencies, which are in fact the national agencies of the triumphant imperial powers of the nineteenth century, traditionally organized their news gathering through cooperation and the establishment of exclusive links with national agencies in countries around the world, a stability which was broken after the First World War. The primacy of Western institutions in the field of global news and the way it was reflected in news content started to be challenged in the 1970s in the context of decolonization in what came to be known as the New World Information and Communication Order (NWICO) debate, in which the creation of national news agencies in Third World countries was promoted.

The field of global news is characterized today by the market dominance of fewer organizations that have become stronger after processes of concentration, deregulation, privatization and commercialization of media industries to an unprecedented degree. While the channels for news transmission have expanded and diversified as a consequence of deregulation, the number of organizations that gather the raw material of news has remained strictly limited and their power has comparatively increased in a context where the commercial logic predominates and it is no longer affordable for many news organizations to obtain their own sources. If we remind ourselves that news agencies produce not only raw information but finished pieces of news that are ready to air/print, this prevalence of a few (Western) organizations implies a certain homogenization of international news in more ways than one. News agencies have not only spread the Western media model and the news values of impartiality, objectivity and neutrality across the globe, but have also shaped the news content, either indirectly, by the imposition of what is considered newsworthy, which areas are given priority, from what angle are events portrayed (their vast agenda-setting powers); or directly, in the provision of journalistic products to their subscribers.

It is important not to underestimate this power and to recognize the determining role of the market, and of the commercial logic, within the journalistic field: on the one hand, it is very unlikely that an event will be reported in a news bulletin if no images are available; on the other, the famous chase for scoops in agency journalism and the principle of breaking news has more to do with beating the main competitors and less with the mere objective of reporting fast on an important event and making it known to the world. In this context, Pierre Bourdieu has indicated two factors that structurally shape the journalistic field. The first refers to 'competition for the newest news', which becomes paramount in a field that is based on the production of such a highly perishable good as the news. The second, utterly paradoxical factor, according to Bourdieu, is the permanent surveillance to which journalists subject their competitors' activities (1998: 71–72). Both elements are in fact closely related: 'actually, a high proportion of the scoops so avidly sought in the battle for customers is destined to remain unknown as such to readers or viewers. Only competitors will see them, since journalists are the only ones who read all the newspapers' (1998: 71–72). In this way, following Bourdieu, competition, rather than favouring originality and diversity, tends to generate uniformity. In news agencies the culture of the scoop is exacerbated by the nature of their function in providing breaking news to their clients 24/7. In addition, news agencies closely monitor not only their competitors' coverage, but also how many news items (both from themselves and from competitors) are picked up and reproduced by subscribing news organizations, and are thus subject to a continuous pressure for commercial success.

For Boyd-Barrett, the study of news agencies confirms that globalization is Westernization: 'News agencies contribute to the homogenization of global culture in form and in source, while greatly multiplying the texts available within these standardized discourses' (Boyd-Barrett, 1997: 143). Others have emphasized the primacy of Anglo-American ideologies in the field of global news (Marchetti, 2002; Paterson, 1998). While all media organizations are influenced by the dominance of the major news agencies, which shape the field of global news in important ways, their direct dependency on them for news sources significantly varies. More powerful news organizations, especially in rich countries, usually have the necessary resources to maintain international correspondents and to send reporters abroad, and thus possess their own sources of information – in spite of a dominant trend towards cutting these costs, limiting the presence of the media abroad and increasing the dependence on news agencies. Less powerful institutions, especially media organizations in poorer countries, are more dependent on the news provided by the news agencies. Thus, the international section of Third World newspapers is typically constituted, almost exclusively, of agency reports. On the other hand, dependency of media organizations on agency news increases in the case of news about distant Third World countries and in the case of international crises such as natural disasters and war.

Examining the role of media coverage of war has been a way of understanding the special significance of the media in constructing reality and promoting what Ulrich Beck describes as the experience of a globalized world. For Beck, 'globality means that from now on nothing which happens on our planet is only a limited local event; all inventions, victories and catastrophes affect the whole world, and we must reorient and reorganize our lives and actions, our organizations and institutions, along a "local–global" axis' (2000: 11–12). The media's role in promoting globality is nowhere more crucial than in war coverage. Beck refers to Martin Shaw's distinction between wars until the end of the East–West conflict and contemporary wars, in which 'potential or actual involvement through the mass media means that wars take place worldwide' (2000: 91). Thus, in certain cases, we can speak of media generation and construction of the global significance of a local military conflict and, even more notoriously, global political crises may be constituted 'even where these are wholly or largely lacking, if there is a world-wide *perception* of a large-scale violation of human life and globally legitimate principles that is largely dependent on media coverage obtained' (Shaw, quoted in Beck, 2000: 92).

The role of the media in generating perceptions which in turn determine the very real events they purport to describe serves as a concrete illustration of Giddens' remark that media do not mirror realities, but shape them in important ways, and of Castells' notion of real virtuality. This can also be illustrated with reference to war coverage by the global news agencies. News agencies have made it their job to be present where no one else can be and to provide a stream of continuous and accurate information in cases in which alternative sources of information are severely limited. However, as Chris Paterson has shown for the case of the Bosnian war, the news agencies' mandate and their privileged place as chroniclers of the war embraced an irresolvable paradox: the war they covered became what the news agencies reported it to be. Thus, Paterson asserts,

> the war news agencies manufactured for the world was the very war they covered. News agencies could report only a small portion of the Bosnian civil war, those portions involving dramatic events occurring within the reach of agency journalists. But that war, the war of singular, seemingly unconnected dramas in a few locations, became the war known to the world, the war the world reacted to, and thus, the war the journalists themselves would continue to focus their efforts upon despite the knowledge of a much larger, much more complex, all but unknown war underway just out of their reach.
>
> (1997: 150–51)

The commercial logic and the market exercise a determining role within the journalistic field. However, the important symbolic value of information should not be disregarded. Pierre Bourdieu described the cultural field as an economy in reverse, where the economic principle is subverted by an autonomous principle, according to which works can become consecrated, i.e. acquire symbolic value and prestige beyond and often against economic success. In spite of the prevalence of commercial factors and of its strong subordination to market forces, the journalistic field is not essentially divergent from this, as the continued predominance of a non-economic principle embodied in the symbolic value of information, which is pivotal in shaping and in determining participation in the public sphere, demonstrates. This is why both governments and profit-making organizations like the news agencies themselves have often invested in maintaining global networks which cannot guarantee economic returns. This is also why news agencies, with their wide agenda-setting powers, were and have remained the most important players in the field of global news.

Thus, regular government subsidies have been used to finance media services which are fundamentally uneconomic. The latter fact is not just a feature of one particular agency, but a structural characteristic of the field of global news: the maintenance of global services for the gathering of information is not economically profitable. The federated Western press has not been prepared to pay for the extremely elevated costs of global information services, and has continuously pushed for low subscription rates. In both organizations Agence France-Presse (AFP) and Reuters it is rather the consideration that news provision is an important public service that has determined the maintenance and expansion of global news services.[1] The French government has provided AFP with the necessary economic backing and, as we will see below, in the case of Reuters it is the unprecedented surplus generated by the development of its economic services that has financed its media services.

In the sections that follow, the history of the main European news agencies (Reuters and Agence Havas/France-Presse) is related to two key periods of globalization in the second half of the nineteenth and twentieth centuries, while recent trends in the field of global news, and especially the appearance of new key actors which challenge the traditional role of news agencies as news sources (channels of continuous information, internet news services), are also approached.

Modern journalism and the birth of the news agency

Modern journalism developed in the middle of the nineteenth century with a burgeoning proliferation of the written press and of the number of readers, as the newspaper became the first mass cultural medium of modernity. The year 1836, which was when Émile Girardin created *La Presse*, conceived of as a politically neutral, colourless, information-based paper, is generally highlighted as signalling its birth. The link to information and no longer to opinion is an important feature of the modern newspaper which, as Dean de la Motte has noted, 'simultaneously and paradoxically seeks to make itself invisible *and* foreground its own materiality *as commodity* (1999: 142, original emphasis). At the same time, advertising made it possible to lower subscription prices and provided the necessary autonomy from the political sphere. However, *La Presse* can be considered more like a precursor, because the mass readership that is another structural characteristic of the modern journalistic field could not be reached until after the creation of *Le Petit Journal* in 1863, which became the greatest emblem of the popular press. *Le Petit Journal* could for the first time be purchased in the streets for a *sou*, introducing a further reduction in price. It was explicitly a non-political paper: to lower production costs it avoided paying the stamp duty required in order to publish political and economic news. *Le Petit Journal* found its content in the everyday life of the streets of Paris and thrived from the enormous popularity of the *roman-feuilleton* and the *fait-divers*. While the former, a serialized novel, introduced fiction into the realms of everyday life, the latter, which covered a wide variety of subjects from crimes to natural disasters or small scandals (Schwartz, 1998: 36), emphasized the fantastic events of ordinary city life and made reality look like fiction. In 1870 *Le Petit Journal* printed nearly 600,000 issues to cover the Troppman affaire,[2] and in 1886 it reached a circulation of 1 million, which was totally unprecedented twenty-five years earlier, when none of the French dailies printed more than 50,000 issues (Palmer, 1983). Britain saw a similar development with the appearance of penny dailies, led by the *Daily Telegraph*, which by 1861 was selling over 140,000 copies, over twice that of *The Times*, five times more expensive. By the turn of the century, the most notable product of the new popular journalism, the *Daily Mail* (founded in 1896), reached a circulation of one million at the height of the Boer war excitement (Read, 1999: 21, 78).

The new mercantile character of factual information is nowhere more visible than in the creation of the news agencies, commercial organizations which were set up by experienced businessmen to gather and sell information when it became a valuable commodity. Charles Havas opened Bureau Havas, which translated foreign newspapers for the French media, in 1832. In 1835 his translation agency was transformed into the first news agency, Agence Havas, now gathering its own news as well as translating articles published by the foreign press. From the beginning, Havas used widely the developing telegraphic network, acquiring the monopoly of non-governmental telegraphy in France. Its news started to appear in the newspapers in 1853 under the title 'Dépêches télégraphiques privées' and covered especially foreign news, although they did not become generalized until several decades later. Meanwhile, Julius Reuter, who worked as sub-editor in Agence Havas in 1848, started his own agency in London in 1851, just when the telegraphic link with the European continent was about to be opened. The American agency Associated Press and the German Wolff had also just been established in 1848 and 1849 respectively. The new penny press, both in France and in Britain, readily subscribed to the information services of the recently created news agencies to satisfy people's growing appetite for the latest news. In fact, Havas soon developed in France a unique position as main provider of information to other media organizations, especially marked in the case of the provincial press, which depended heavily on its Parisian news. In Britain the situation was different, as *The Times* had already its own network of information-gathering services including foreign correspondents. *The Times* did not subscribe to Reuters until 1859, and even then it sought to maintain independent coverage through its own correspondents. However, the advantage of the news agencies in obtaining fast information from distant places had been sufficiently demonstrated in the middle of the 1850s with the Crimean war, when both Havas and Reuter made use of their agents in strategic places like St Petersburg, Vienna and Constantinople.

If the structural conditions for the development of an autonomous journalistic field seem to have been created first in France, both in institutional terms and because of the earlier attainment of a mass readership, the discursive practices that constitute the norm in modern journalism were not. As Jean Chalaby (1996) has argued, the modern conception of news as description of fact is embodied in two genres of Anglo-American origin: the news report and the interview. Both emphasize factual description and provide a sense of immediacy to the narrated events. Moreover, the report, with its conciseness and economy of words, was ideally suited to the telegraphic style at a time when the technology was still very expensive. These forms were gradually introduced in the French press during the second half of the nineteenth century and became dominant by its end, revealing the mixture of fact and fiction – of literature and journalism – characteristic of the popular press as a transitional form. According to Chalaby, Parisian dailies began to employ 'reporters' in the 1870s, and the English word was adopted to designate the new breed of journalists which still occupied a position of clear inferiority with respect to the journalists who did not merely 'consider facts as facts', but who saw it as their task to provide plausible interpretations (1996: 309). But by the end of the century reporters, thought to better serve 'the recently developed taste for precise information' (Schwartz, 1998: 40), started to be more popular than established *chroniqueurs* such as *Le Petit Journal*'s Timothy Trimm. The interview, which Michael Schudson characterizes by its American-ness as well as its modernity (1995: 76), became a common journalistic practice in America by the 1860s and spread to Britain and France during the early 1880s, first appearing in the pages of *Le Petit Journal* in 1884 and not becoming fully accepted by the British until after 1900 (Chalaby, 1996: 312; Schudson, 1995: 48–49, 72–93; Schwartz, 1998: 40–41).

According to Michael Palmer, the growing importance given to facts and to reportage is a fundamental aspect of the transformation of the French press during the period 1860–80 (1983: 14). The popular press became better informed and more factual in character and, from the abolition of stamp duty in 1870, no longer needed to avoid political and economic information. A radical break in style was introduced in the 1880s by the new *presse d'information*, represented by the newspaper *Le Matin* (created 1884), which employed many British and American journalists and provided accurate 'American-style' factual information without commentary, while also exploiting the 'human interest' dimension in domestic and foreign news. *Le Matin* defined itself as a 'journal d'informations télégraphiques personnelles et vraies', and possessed its own special cable linking Paris and London, publishing last-minute news from the whole world (Palmer, 1983: 96). Parliamentary and court reporters, already an existing asset of important American and British dailies, became widespread in France as well. They informed without colouring the facts, even in the case of politics, which now became one more item in the newspaper. Reportage also extended to all the domains that could interest avid newspaper readers: sports, entertainment and the arts, tourism, urban, provincial and international news, from local scandals and petty crime to international conflicts and wars. The end of the nineteenth century marks the era of the great reportage, of the special correspondent and the war reporter, who brought fresh news from international conflicts to the great Western news centres. Important newspapers (British first and, by the turn of the century, French too) also started to send their own correspondents to cover great international confrontations such as the Franco-Prussian war of 1870–71, the two Boer wars (1881, 1899–1902) and the Russo-Japanese war (1904–5). In this context, in relation to the interest created in Europe by the Cuban war (1898) and the siege of Beijing (1900), Palmer speaks of the globalization of the event (1983: 213).

Modern journalism is global in scope

The birth of modern journalism was also the birth of global journalism. As we have indicated above, the telegraph made possible for newspapers to select events according to their significance and no longer to where they took place and the newspaper became a palimpsest where different events from the most diverse places coexisted, thus creating an experience of global simultaneity. On the other hand, the faster that information about distant events could reach European readers, the stronger the demand grew for the latest information on a daily basis.

The demand for fast and reliable information from all over the globe was not only related to the need for an up to date knowledge of world events generated by the new press of information, but also to the political and economic developments of modern globalization (which David Held et al. roughly situate between 1850 and 1945), a period marked by the enormous acceleration of the spread and entrenchment of global networks and flows, under the control of European powers (Held et al., 1999: 421). Under the Western empires, global political and military relations expanded and the intensity of international links in areas like trade, investment and migration greatly increased. In this context, the significance of the telegraph, which led to the establishment of a global infrastructure for communications for the first time, is therefore no less important than that of steam.

The expansion of the telegraph network is directly linked to the emergence and consolidation of the news agencies, which became specialized in providing fast and accurate telegraphic information not only to their media clients, but also to commercial clients and to governments. Invented in 1833, the telegraph was maintained as a state monopoly in most European countries except Britain, where the telegraphic network was developed by private companies with generous government subsidies. In France, in 1850, the state made its network available to private clients, the most important of which was Agence Havas. The 1850s saw the quick development of the European cable network. The first undersea cable, linking Dover and Calais, was opened in 1851, allowing investors to know the values of the London stock exchange on the same day. By 1854, the French telegraphic network was 9,200 km in total, linking Paris to Brussels, Vienna, London and Madrid (Palmer, 1983: 42). However, in the early days, telegraphic links remained discontinuous, and rail, steamships and pigeons were still widely used for the transmission of information.

By the end of the 1850s, although European news still predominated, the news agencies started to respond to the growing demand for news about the wider world by improving their infrastructures to provide news material that sometimes took a long time to reach Europe. Thus, in 1859 Reuters started its 'Special India and China Service', although news of the surrender of Beijing to British and French troops on 13 October 1860 took nearly two months to reach London. By 1861 news from Australia, New Zealand and South Africa had begun to feature regularly in the Reuters file (Read, 1999: 37). A special relationship with America was also soon developed, which led to the 1862 news exchange agreement between Reuters and the Associated Press of New York, and London and Reuters were placed in the unique privileged position as main channel and prime supplier of American news to the European continent. In 1858 a first transatlantic cable was briefly operational, but the first successful cable to America was not laid until 1866.

Telegraphic networks, which followed the geography of empire, soon linked the most distant parts of the world to the metropolitan centres. During the 1860s and 1870s British possessions in Asia and Africa were linked to London: India was reached overland across Russia and under sea via Alexandria and Aden in 1870; Hong Kong was reached from India in 1871, Shanghai and Tokyo in 1873. Australia was linked with India via Ceylon in 1872. The 1870s are characterized by the consolidation of British dominance of the submarine cable system, aided by technological improvements and the active policy of the British government, so that by 1900 the British owned 72 per cent of the approximately 190,000 miles of submarine cable in the world and established themselves as information hegemons (Headrick, 1981: 160, 162; Hugill, 1999: 28). British investments and expansion of the global cable system responded not only to imperial administrative, economic and business needs, but also to political and strategic concerns, which determined the construction of an 'All-Red Route' linking the globe with a cable passing only through British territories, which was completed in 1902 (Headrick, 1981: 162–63).[3]

London's position as global news centre was not only due to its important role in providing American news to the European continent, but also to British control of the global cable network and is echoed today by its centrality as headquarters of the two biggest global television news agencies, Reuters Television and Associated Press Television. Thus, in spite of no longer being at the geographical centre of a global network of telecommunications (a hegemony that was not successfully challenged until the 1950s with the use of newer communications technologies), London's centrality in global news markets has endured, pointing to the continued relevance of the key strategic position it developed early on between the two biggest information markets – the US and Europe – and to the importance of the symbolic value of information beyond purely economic and material factors.

The global expansion of the telegraphic network during the second half of the nineteenth century was paralleled by the expansion of the news agencies' international infrastructure to respond to new informative demands. From the beginning, news agencies formed international alliances to ensure global coverage. A first agreement for news exchange between Havas, Wolff and Reuters dates from 1859. This, and subsequent agreements which also included the American partner Associated Press, effectively divided the world into main zones of influence for each agency. Havas' territories included France and the Mediterranean region, the French Empire and, from 1890, also South America. Wolff kept Germany, Scandinavia and Eastern Europe, while Reuters retained control of Britain and Holland, the British Empire and the Far East. Associated Press' areas were the United States, Canada, Alaska, and parts of the Caribbean and Central America.[4] Within their own territories agencies collected news either by developing their own networks or by establishing links with other national agencies.

The scheme for territorial division and cooperation between news agencies was soon complemented by the expansion of each agency's own European network. Reuters had opened its own offices in the main European capitals by 1870, partly to provide European news to its American partner, Associated Press. Havas was forced to respond, also due to the increasing competition with newspapers like *The Times* and the *New York Herald*, which possessed their own European network of correspondents, by establishing its own agents in the main news centres of Europe: approximately ten between 1875 and 1885 (Palmer, 1983: 113).

Correspondents and offices were also established in important capitals in non-European news markets. By 1861 Reuters was claiming agents at the main ports of India, China, Japan, Australia and New Zealand, and at the intermediate ports of Pont de Galle (Ceylon), Alexandria and Malta (Read, 1999: 62). Its first office outside Europe opened in Alexandria in 1865. A Bombay office opened in 1866, while in 1878 a general manager for Australia and New Zealand was appointed. In 1876 a full-time agent was sent to Cape Town, which was connected by cable in 1887. In addition, after the laying of a cable across the South Atlantic in 1874, Reuters and Havas established joint offices in Brazil, Argentina and Uruguay. European predominance in the news markets of the French and British empires was to become increasingly challenged, from the beginning of the twentieth century, by the American agencies, especially after the creation of United Press International in 1907, which entered into fierce competition with Associated Press. The breach of the principle of the exclusivity of news distribution in the allocated territories by the American agencies, which started to sell their news directly to the European press, the creation of new international alliances for news exchange between newspapers and the polarization of European diplomacy finally led to the abandonment of the territorial divisions between news agencies in the interwar years.

The news agencies not only developed a global infrastructure for news production and distribution, which brought the most distant events to newspaper readers ever faster and more accurately, they also made it their task to extend their values of impartiality and objectivity[5] and discursive practices based on factual description worldwide. We have seen how 'American-style' journalism had been established as the dominant form in France by the end of the nineteenth century. The Western news agencies further spread the style and news values of modern journalism to the rest of the world, teaching national agencies how to participate in global news markets,[6] as well as creating their own international infrastructures for news production in their respective territories.

The present phase of globalization

Oliver Boyd-Barrett and Terhi Rantanen (1998) have characterized the global news agencies as agents of globalization. The above overview of the emergence and development of the modern journalistic field and the news agencies in the context of accelerated globalization in the second half of the nineteenth century has illustrated the central role of the latter not only in disseminating consciousness of the world as a whole (Robertson, 1992: 8), but also in the development of material infrastructures for the production and circulation of information worldwide. News agencies have had a no less central role in the current phase of globalization, from the end of the 1960s, which is characterized by a further intensification of the processes of global interconnectedness. As will be shown in this section, news agencies, again at the forefront of the technological developments that are central to the new phase of globalization, have been instrumental in creating the very conditions that make global interconnectedness possible.

From the 1960s, information technology and satellite communications provoked a revolution which is similar in scope to that of the telegraph a century earlier. An unprecedented quantitative multiplication of the amount of information that could be circulated was matched by an equally crucial qualitative change which saw the introduction of customization and interactivity, giving users the freedom to individually select what they needed from an immense information pool. Manuel Castells speaks of a massive communication explosion which, led by television, has spread throughout the world during the past three decades, in which mass communication has given way to segmentation and individualization, and one-way communication has been substituted by interaction between sender and receiver (2000: 361). In turn, in the second half of the 1990s, globalized, customized mass media and computer-mediated communication gave birth to a new communication system which is characterized by the integration of different media and by its interactive potential (2000: 394).

News agencies were among the first organizations to explore the possibilities of information technology, which in the course of the 1970s made it possible to end the division between journalists (who wrote the reports) and technician telegraphists (who introduced them into the wire) and concentrate all the tasks in the figure of the journalist, who now typed the news directly into the system. Information technology also provided the means to customize information and make it available to clients selectively at the switch of a button. However, like a century earlier with the telegraph, news agencies were not only important users of new technologies but, more crucially, played a determining role in their development and thus in shaping contemporary globalization in important ways. This can best be illustrated by looking in some detail at the development of Reuters' economic services from the 1960s, which radically changed the nature and role of this organization.

Economic and financial services had been important in the news agencies since their inception, as the potential of fast and accurate information for trade and investment was immediately realized in a time of expanding global markets. However, they had always occupied a subordinate position with respect to media services, and financial journalists did not possess the prestige of general news reporters. In Reuters, the situation started to change at the end of the 1960s, after a decade of increasing uncertainty and precarious finances. Massive investments were made for the use of new information technologies and to expand financial services, destined particularly for Western countries. By 1968 the revenue obtained from Reuters Economic Services had overtaken that of its General News Division, an overall figure which was determined by revenues from financial services in North America and, especially, Europe. By 1973, the much greater profit-making potential of the economic services with respect to general news had been structurally recognized (Read, 1999: 350–51). However, the transformation which took place was not only related to the growing importance of financial information, but also to the adoption of new interactive technologies which allowed customers to use information selectively according to their needs: computer-based products which started to make real-time information instantly available to bankers and brokers. In 1973 Reuters launched its most important innovation: the Reuter Monitor Money Rates service, effectively creating a virtual marketplace which functions in real time. Monitor introduced for the first time an interactive database in which clients worldwide could contribute their foreign exchange and money rates, information which would be made instantly available to recipients. In 1981 a new dealing service was launched in which subscribers did not only have access to the information but could also engage in financial transactions. If we remind ourselves that Castells defined a global economy as 'an economy with the capacity to work as a unit in real time, or chosen time, on a planetary scale' (2000: 101), then Reuters was instrumental in creating this economy.

In his history of Reuters, Donald Read has characterized the development of its economic services as the making of the new Reuters. He also hints at the paradox that it is an established, old company which has led such a crucial development in the use of the latest information technologies (1999: 402). The fact that it was Reuters, the old agency of the British Empire, and not a new US company that introduced these electronic information technologies may have been a contingency. However, what is not contingent is that Reuters benefits from a long-standing tradition in the gathering and transmission of information worldwide and that since their creation news agencies have characteristically been at the forefront of the latest developments in the very technologies that have made globalization possible.

Global news agencies

During the nineteenth century and the first half of the twentieth, the big news agencies were not in fact, beyond their imperial connections, global entities in a strict sense. They rather established transnational networks on the basis of alliances with their biggest competitors which, as we have seen, effectively divided the world into areas of influence and substituted competition for cooperation. In addition, within their allocated territories, the global agencies often instituted news exchange treaties with national agencies, rather than develop their own networks. These agreements implied not only that agencies relied on other organizations for news production, but also that they could not sell their services directly to the media. Generally, the domestic bases of the global news agencies remained very strong both in terms of news production and in terms of revenue, but their world coverage was incomplete and dependent on the networks of other agencies, even in the most important international news markets.

With increased worldwide competition in the interwar years and a changing power balance between agencies, the agreements that the big players had reached and subsequently renewed in the previous decades lost their essence. The American agencies, Associated Press and United Press International, competing to reach new markets, developed from the 1920s and 1930s aggressive policies in Latin America and Asia and started to target the European markets directly. Associated Press was the older of the two and an established partner in the news exchange agreements with the European agencies, where it was nevertheless not recognized as equal until 1927, when the differential it was obliged to pay to the other agencies was abolished. From 1934, a new agreement with Reuters left AP finally free to compete anywhere in the world and ended the division of the globe into exclusive zones of influence. However, the historic territorial divisions and a legacy of dependency on other agencies were not fully abandoned. While the American agencies started to expand their worldwide networks early on, a substantial effort on the part of the European agencies to gain international clients, develop their global infrastructures and cut back their dependency on other agencies was not undertaken until the 1960s. This would lead, towards the end of the twentieth century, to the establishment of true supranational entities for the gathering and transmission of news and, as Boyd-Barrett and Rantanen point out, to the diminished scope for control of international news services within national markets (2004: 36).

In 1949, five years after its foundation, Agence France-Presse was growing and recuperating some of Havas' old strongholds: it distributed its news services in forty countries, it had regained old positions in Latin America and was progressing in Japan, while it dominated the market in Belgium,

Switzerland, Portugal, Turkey, Greece and Lebanon. However, it did not distribute its news in Britain, Scandinavia or the US. AFP's worldwide expansion and its role and presence in Asia were given a new turn with the opening of the Beijing bureau in 1958. In Africa, AFP maintained its old links with the Francophone territories, while developing new ones with the independent English-speaking nations from the beginning of the 1960s, finding a ready market willing to diversify its sources of information and break its dependency on the old colonial power. Only Reuters would develop a comparable network in black Africa, while the American agencies remained largely absent from a market that represented an insignificant part of their revenues (1 per cent in AP's case).

By 1960 AFP was present in 125 countries, transmitting 500,000 words a day and employing a staff of 2,000 journalists and technicians. However, in the US its market was still strictly limited. US subscribers were slow to come. During the Vietnam war, AFP was the only Western agency present at Hanoi, and widely quoted and reproduced by US media. In 1972, the *Washington Post* and *Los Angeles Times*, whose service was distributed to another 207 US newspapers, joined AFP, two months after one of the biggest scoops of its history, when it was the only agency to inform of the death of Israeli hostages in the hands of terrorists during the Munich Olympic Games. AFP did not develop its own independent service for news gathering in the US until 1995, remaining until then dependent on its American news from AP in exchange for news about France and Francophone Africa.

Unlike the other global agencies, AFP has not substantially diversified into non-media products and remains thus inevitably linked to the structural shortages of information gathering, which rarely makes profit in a market in which the price of information is often kept below production costs.[7] However, there has been in the past decades an important development towards the diversification of its media products, both in terms of thematic specialization and in the introduction of new media products. AFP has reputedly one of the best sport services, which was developed from 1955 with the explicit aim of turning it 'into what the economic service is for Reuters' (Huteau and Ullmann, 1992: 272). AFP's most important venture in this context is its international photographic service, which it has offered since 1985, and through which the agency finally established itself within the elusive US market, gaining the subscriptions of the biggest American dailies. Today AFP employs 2,000 people worldwide, of which 1,250 are journalists, and has a presence in 165 countries (it has established bureaus in 110, while the other 50 are covered by part-time correspondents or stringers), producing a file of 400,000 to 600,000 words a day in six languages. It has managed to maintain, with a much smaller economic base than AP or Reuters, a place as one of the leading global agencies.

In 1945, Reuters employed 2,000 staff worldwide. It had large offices in 23 countries and small bureaus in another 19. It supplied its news directly to subscribers in 14 countries, but in another 31 distribution still took place through the national agencies. Most subscribing media were from countries within the British Empire (Read, 1999: 308). For Reuters, the path towards achieving an independent worldwide presence was, in the first place, one of breaking with the old special relationships that had been established with agencies of the formal and informal British Empire. India, its most profitable market for decades, withdrew from a Commonwealth partnership. In Japan, the Japanese agency Kyodo took over the Reuters English-language service in 1953. In South Africa, the preferential relationship with the South African Press Association was ended in 1966, when Reuters became fully autonomous in producing its own South African news. In Australia, Reuters assumed main responsibility for both general news and economic information in 1977. The end of Reuters' special relationship with the media in the countries of the old empire was paralleled by its expansion into new territories in South East Asia, where competition with the American agencies and AFP was strong, as well as into Latin America and Africa, both English and French speaking.

Reuters also needed to break with its reliance on the other global agencies, with whom it had long sustained news exchange agreements, and especially with its dependency on American news from AP. In the 1940s and 1950s, Reuters' position in the US was mainly one of secondary news supplier. Its news-gathering network in the country was expanded during the 1950s to become the biggest overseas Reuters operation, with about 50 full-time staff and 150 stringers (Read, 1999: 304). However, its dependence on AP did not disappear until 1967, when in response to AP's dramatic price increase, Reuters assumed the full weight of news reporting from the US, with 105 full-time staff. Collaboration with Dow Jones for American market information was ended at the same time. Reuters was nevertheless not to achieve a prominent presence in the US until the end of the 1970s.

Europe emerged after the Second World War as the main region for revenue, and offices were opened in Berlin, Hamburg, Bonn and Frankfurt. From 1960, Reuters started to relax its traditional ties with the national news agencies and distribute its news directly to subscribing media. A German-language news service edited in Bonn was launched in 1971, after the end of the connection with the German news agency Deutsche Presse-Agentur, while a French-language service was offered to France, Belgium and Switzerland. Today, Reuters possesses 2,400 editorial staff in 197 bureaus worldwide, which serve approximately 130 countries, publishing daily over eight million words in six languages.

But Reuters' transformation has come about not from its expanding global networks and from diversification of its media services (the acquisition of UPI's news picture business in 1984 and of the television news-film agency Visnews, renamed Reuters Television, in 1992), but from the development of new technologies of data-processing for the transmission of economic information which, as we have seen, became its main profit-generating services at the end of the 1960s. Its expanding economic services placed

Reuters by 1980 in a leading market position, reaching a similar level of revenues as the market leader AP, while AFP was left far behind by the two Anglo-American giants – revenues for that year were $150 million for AP, $140 million for Reuter and $70 million for AFP (Huteau and Ullmann, 1992: 415). By 1995, Reuters, with total revenues of £2,703 million, had almost twelve times AP's £230 million turnover (Boyd-Barrett, 1998: 28). Significantly, the origin of Reuters' revenues is very different from that of the American agencies, which are characterized by their strong domestic base and their essentially American nature. Thus, in 1977 AP's foreign income amounted to only about 20 per cent of its revenue; conversely, Reuters earned only 16 per cent of its revenue from the United Kingdom (Read, 1999: 477). This is why, according to Read, in terms of revenue Reuters can be considered the most global of the global agencies. However, in 1989 only 7 per cent of Reuters' total revenues came from media products, which reveals the subordinated place that general news now occupies within globalized communication markets.

The move towards the establishment of true transnational organizations also implied a process of decentralization that took place during the 1980s, which was designed to make global agencies more responsive to regional needs and culminated with the transfer of editorial and managerial powers to the agencies' regional headquarters. In 1986 AFP transferred its foreign desks away from Paris: a Latin American desk was established in Washington (which later returned to Paris and is now finally shared between the new regional headquarters in Montevideo and Paris); an English desk in between Hong Kong, Paris and Washington; a German desk in Bonn; and a desk for the Middle East in Nicosia. Reuters ended London's global editorial control in 1982, when responsibilities started to be shared between London, Hong Kong and later also New York.

There is little doubt that in the course of the second half of the twentieth century the news agencies have realized the objectives that were established at their creation a century earlier and become truly global transnational entities, with worldwide networks for news production and circulation. However, it still remains to be seen whether they have sufficiently disengaged themselves from their national and/or regional base in their news production. Read has stressed how, from being the agency of the British Empire and providing news from the 'British point of view', Reuters has had, after the Second World War, to progressively address clients as a world agency, bearing in mind all the possible news angles as well as news markets. On the other hand, Boyd-Barrett has pointed out that Reuters, and maybe to a lesser extent AFP, have had a greater motivation to respond to international news requirements than the American agencies, which have very wealthy domestic bases (1980: 24). However, the fact that by far the most important news markets are Western also weights powerfully on the character of the global news agencies.[8] Fundamental criticisms about the representation of Third World countries were already raised in the UNESCO debate for a

New World Information and Communication Order (NWICO) that took place in the 1970s. Today, the appearance of non-Western media like Al-Jazeera in the field of global news poses a new challenge to this issue.

Alternative news agencies

The arguments put forward in the context of the NWICO debate, which culminated in the 1980 MacBride report, encouraged Third World countries to set up their own national agencies and to establish regional news exchange mechanisms to counter the effects of Western dominance in media flows. However, when the ideological principles that determined coverage were not fundamentally questioned, the newly emerged national agencies ended up replicating the schemes of the global agencies and privileging the same type of news – elites over civil society, urban over rural contexts, politics and economics over culture, social issues and education – and journalistic values. By contrast, the notion of an alternative news agency is used to designate an institution if the purpose for which it was set up, as well as its functions, are different from the dominant model, which implies going beyond the familiar context of transmitting 'impartial', 'balanced', 'objective' and 'neutral' news reports (Musa, 1997: 126–27).

Inter Press Service (IPS) is the most significant alternative global agency, the first organization of its kind that has established a worldwide network of journalists and become the largest supplier of information about the less developed nations. IPS was founded in 1964 as an information bridge between Europe and Latin America. Its focus was subsequently broadened to the issues concerning less developed regions generally, and its emphasis became the promotion of horizontal, South–South information flows (Giffard, 1998: 191). In contrast to the Western agencies, IPS focus is not on breaking news, or even events as such, but on in-depth views of major stories which give explanations of how and why events occur. Its thematic scope also widely differs from the dominant norm, concentrating on issues such as the gap between the rich and the poor, human rights and democracy, international trade negotiations, refugees and international migration patterns, environmental protection and sustainable development, etc. Its stated objectives are 'equal gender representation and balanced representation of ethnic diversity and geographical distribution', and the organization is further dedicated to 'promoting democratic participation in social, economic and political life, the full involvement of the countries of the South in international policy-making and the full empowerment of women in the development process'. As we will see in more detail in the following chapters, IPS' editorial policy also implies a very different approach to language and translation: the significance of minority languages is recognized and their role in facilitating communication between peoples, rather than the economic principle associated with news provision in the languages of the most important markets, becomes the main concern. IPS has global services in two languages, Spanish and English, and provides regional selections in fourteen other languages (Arabic, Dutch, Finnish, French, German, Italian, Japanese, Kiswahili, Mandarin, Nepali, Portuguese, Swedish, Thai and Turkish).

IPS is an international cooperative of journalists and has its world headquarters in Rome, with regional editorial centres in Africa (Johannesburg), Asia-Pacific (Bangkok), Europe (Berlin) and Latin America (Montevideo). It offers about thirty daily news reports (typically longer than mainstream news agency reports) in the World Service, a selection of which is translated into other languages, and also provides coverage of major international conferences in its newspaper *TerraViva*, produced daily at each of the major UN conferences, as well as at the World Social Forum. IPS employs today over 250 journalists (most of them stringers), has 14 full-time bureaus and a presence in 150 countries, producing daily around 112,000 words in 16 languages. The organization's worldwide network is at present, nevertheless, a fraction of what it used to be before a long decade of deep financial crisis:

> The same process of globalization that shaped the mission and editorial policies of IPS in recent years precipitated a crisis in its operations. Funding for IPS comes from three main sources: sale of its news services to media and other users; grants and projects paid for by outside organizations; and carrier services. All three revenue streams have dwindled. By comparison with traditional international agencies such as the Associated Press or Reuters, IPS is a shoestring operation. At its most affluent, in 1992, the agency's annual budget totalled $15 million. By 1997, this had shrunk to $5.8 million, resulting in severe reductions in expenditure in every region.
>
> (Giffard, 1998: 198)

The crisis was met with a decentralization of management to the regions and the cutting of costs, which deeply affected the news service: the number of countries with permanent bureaus dropped from 44 in 1995 to 41 in 1996; the number of permanent staff from 192 to 140; the number of stringers from 351 to 233; and output was limited to 30 news features a day. However, despite the cuts, IPS seems to have retained most of its major subscribers which, in 1996, included 615 newspapers and magazines, 79 news agencies and databases and 65 broadcast media, as well as another 549 NGOs and other institutions (Giffard, 1998: 199, 194). During the past decade, IPS' network has further been reduced by at least 50 per cent.

Because of its radically different approach to news provision, IPS does not directly compete with the big agencies, but rather provides supplementary coverage. Moreover, as Anthony Giffard points out, the background news that it offers is not particularly attractive to market-driven commercial media and, as a consequence, two-thirds of its subscribers are in developing regions that have fewer and less affluent media (1998: 200). In addition, as Oliver Boyd-Barrett and Daya Thussu observe, IPS' focus on processes rather than on spot news as well as its specific editorial angle have been and continue to be an obstacle in penetrating even the major media markets in the Third World, which still largely subscribe to Western canons of journalism. Nevertheless, these authors also emphasize that 'IPS' news service style has helped to change the ways news is defined, gathered and focused, perhaps even influencing practice within the major transnational news agencies, by showing in practice that many areas not considered news-worthy can in fact be so' (1992: 35). It remains to be seen whether a real challenge to mainstream news can come from such a marginal approach based on principles that do not feature high in the field of global news, and whether IPS' influence must remain strictly limited to questioning the Western values of objectivity and neutrality and showing that a different way of news provision is possible.

Recent developments in the field of global news

In the past two decades, the field of global news has undergone processes of concentration and, at the same time, of unprecedented deregulation of com-munication channels. One of the four leading global agencies, the American United Press International, has gone through a long crisis since the 1980s, changing hands several times and gradually losing its role as a major player. A new important development of the 1990s is the appearance of film news agencies. Visnews was transformed into Reuters Television in 1992 and Associated Press Television was launched in 1994. The field of visual news is today dominated by these two major global players. Yet, while it is possible to view global news agencies as comparatively more important than ever before in a context in which many smaller media organizations have had to cut costs and increase their reliance on this type of news sources, the tradi-tional role of the news agency has also been challenged by the appearance of new media organizations and increased competition around practices of news provision that were previously the sole province of the news agencies.

In this context, one of the most significant recent developments in the field of global news is the appearance of channels of continuous information, which have generated not only a quantitative change in the circulation of global news, but also a radical transformation of its form. The most sig-nificant innovator in this context is CNN (Cable News Network), the American commercial satellite channel created in 1980, at a time when most commercial ventures took place in the field of entertainment. In 1980 CNN reached 1 million or 8 per cent of all US television households. In 1984 it was available in 22 nations of Central America and the Caribbean, and international expansion continued to Europe and Africa. By 1992, CNN and CNN International combined reached 119 million households in over 140 countries (Volkmer, 1999: 132–35).

Like the news agencies that pioneered the use of the telegraph in the nineteenth century, CNN benefited from the early use of satellite technology for news transmission and discovered a new potential in the marketability of news, earning a reputation for airing globally attractive mass news events, such as the Challenger explosion and the Tiananmen Square uprising (Volkmer, 1999: 128). CNN successfully introduced an innovative news style based on immediacy, live coverage and breaking news, emphasizing its reliance on factual information and minimizing interpretative commentary and the dramatic and personalized style that had become characteristic of television news. In this sense, the qualitative change brought about by CNN at the end of the twentieth century also resembles the telegraphic news style introduced by the news agencies in the middle of the nineteenth century.

The parallels highlighted above between CNN – or, more generally, continuous information channels – and news agencies are not fortuitous, as there are underlying structural resemblances between the two types of media. Broadcasting 24/7 means that continuous information channels are subject to the same pressures as news agencies to provide accurate information fast, although in this case breaking news reaches the public directly. In addition, channels of continuous information break with Boyd-Barrett's distinction between information wholesalers (the news agencies) and retailers (media organizations addressed to the public), by also selling their news to other media. More generally, it can be argued that channels like CNN make the traditional distinction between national and international events blur and create a world event, a mediatized political event assumed to be of global interest. This was never fully achieved by the news agencies, which have always been based on the principle that international news should be adapted to specific markets, an operation undertaken by both their own editorial desks and subscribing media organizations, which have always enjoyed the freedom to alter the news file and adapt it to their own needs in any way required.

But if continuous information channels offer images and narratives of what are seemingly world events, of interest to international audiences because of their global implications, it is also true that they are Western media, the channels of Western dominance in global communication flows. This dominance has only started to be challenged with the appearance of non-Western players, which have recently acquired a new significance in the global media field. The most important of these is Al-Jazeera. This pan-Arab channel of continuous information was founded in 1996 under the auspices of the Emir of Qatar, Sheikh Hamad bin Khalifa. It profited from the closing down of the BBC's Arabic Television network, from which it drew technical infrastructure and personnel. Assuming a pledge for objective reporting and contrasted points of view, Al-Jazeera initiated a revolution in the Arab world by breaking with a regional tradition that had subordinated the media to the government and by introducing new democratic practices in broadcasting. The channel was controversial from the start, giving a space to the points of view of Israelis, Chechens, members of organizations like Hamas and Al-Qaeda, and individuals like Colonel Gaddafi and Saddam

Hussein, who were invited to interviews. It also broadcast talk shows that tackled political and social taboos never confronted before, and involved its audience in new ways. Its prestige in the Arab world was well established by 2000, when the channel achieved significant scoops in its coverage of the Palestinian Intifada. But Al-Jazeera's position was to become recognized on the world stage in 2001 after the September 11 attacks, first with its broadcasting of the Bin Laden tapes, later with its exclusive coverage of the war in Afghanistan.[9]

Al-Jazeera's challenge to Western and, more particularly, American dominance in global media flows was expressed in the bombing of its Kabul offices during the war in Afghanistan. Explicitly embracing the media values of objectivity, accuracy and balanced, factual reporting, and modelling itself after the Western media tradition of the BBC (where many of its staff were trained) and CNN (the channel it seeks to imitate and compete with), Al-Jazeera shows nevertheless that a very different, alternative news angle can be followed. It portrays a concealed reality: it displays the images of war and death that no American television network will show, it gives airtime to the people who will be barred from appearing in any other network. In so doing, Al-Jazeera shows that real-time, life television coverage of world events, which has given origin to the belief in a new immediacy, is a mediated immediacy.

Like CNN, Al-Jazeera reaches out to global audiences. Both channels have found a niche in mobile, diasporic audiences which go beyond traditional geographical boundaries and identify a new dimension of the global. Broadcast in all major international hotels, CNN reaches international tourists and travelling professionals, as well as Americans and other Westerners living abroad. Al-Jazeera has become the most important medium for the diasporic Arab community in the West, as well as the most popular television channel in the Middle East. Although predominantly regional in scope, the consequences of its reporting are truly global and the channel is reaching out to new international audiences. In 2003 an English-language website was introduced and, after some delays, an English-language channel was finally inaugurated in November 2006. The launch of this English channel, the purpose of which is to 'communicate with the West in its own language about issues pertaining to the Middle East as a direct, credible, alternative source of information' (Jihad Ballout, quoted in Miles, 2005: 412), constitutes an unprecedented challenge to global Western media dominance.

The news agencies are responding to the erosion of the distinction between wholesale news producers and retailers introduced by the channels of continuous information by addressing their news directly to the public through the internet, which has become an important medium for the integration of text and audio-visual communication. Reuters' website was recently ranked amongst the fifteen world's first digital news media (Muro Benayas, 2006: 147, based on Alexa's site traffic rankings). Information services like Yahoo

News, MSNBC and Google News, and media such as the BBC, CNN and the *New York Times*, occupy the top positions, while Reuters is, by far, the first of the news agencies in the ranking. The blurring of the boundaries and markets of the news agencies and other media is mirrored in the multimedia spaces inaugurated by the internet, which at the beginning of the twenty-first century has revolutionized the field of global news in a no less radical form than the penny press that created modern journalism in the nineteenth century, and the consequences of which are still largely unexplored.

4 Translation in global news agencies

News agencies as translation agencies

This chapter will substantiate the view introduced in Chapter 3 that news agencies can be viewed as vast translation agencies, structurally designed to achieve fast and reliable translations of large amounts of information. It will maintain that translation is of the utmost importance in the news agencies and that it is inseparable from other journalistic practices that intervene in the production of news. Rejecting the naive view that translations are often improvised by people who do not have the necessary training, this chapter will show that the news editor has the specific skills required for the elaboration of such translations, and that the organization of the news agency has been conceived in order to facilitate communication flows between different linguistic communities so as to reach global publics with maximum speed and efficiency.

We saw in the last chapter how news agencies specialized, since their inception, in the provision of international news, initially to domestic markets and later, through alliances with other news organizations worldwide, on a global scale. This implied dealing with a diversity of languages and with translation from the very start. It is not a coincidence that these organizations were created by cosmopolitan, multilingual businessmen: Charles Havas had lived and conducted business in Lisbon, while Paul Julius Reuter was a German who obtained his initial experience of news agency journalism in France before settling in Britain. In fact, as we have seen, before it was transformed into the first news agency in 1835, Agence Havas was a translation agency known as Bureau Havas (1832–35), which provided the French media and business community with translations from the international press. Bureau Havas centralized news translations leaving many freelancers out of work and is the first expression of the growing need for international news from around the world. In the first decades after their inception, news agencies already offered news services in different languages directed at the main Western news markets, and developed global networks which efficiently dealt with linguistic diversity. Agency journalists who pioneered in the expansion of their worldwide networks, managing offices in new regions and serving as agents in the furthest corners of the world, were, very much like the founders themselves, also characterized by their cosmopolitan formation and multilingual skills.[1]

The organization and features of news agencies today with regard to language and translation are not substantially different from what they were in the second half of the nineteenth century. Global news agencies traditionally produce newswires in the major European languages (Reuters and AFP in English, French, Spanish, Portuguese, German – AP does not offer a Portuguese service but produces a Dutch wire), which are the languages of their main news markets. To these only Arabic is a recent addition (launched by Reuters in 1954 and by AFP in 1969).[2] Therefore, news translation into one of these major languages is undertaken by the news agencies themselves. In the case of other languages, it is the subscribing news organizations which assume the task of translating the information provided by the news agencies.

The need to deal with linguistic diversity in news production and the simultaneous circulation of news in different languages make translation an important part of news agency work. But news agencies do not tend to employ translators as such. This is because translation is not conceived as separate from other journalistic tasks of writing up and editing, and is mainly assumed by the news editor, who usually works as part of a desk, where news reports are edited and translated and sent to a specific newswire. Both processes of edition and translation imply the tasks of selection, correction, verification, completion, development or reduction that will give texts the final form in which they appear in the newswire.

Translation is thus an important part of journalistic work and is subject to the same requirements of genre and style that govern journalistic production in general. News organizations employ journalists rather than translators because only the former have the specific skills needed for the job: an experience of journalistic work and a precise knowledge of journalistic genres and style. Even if they are not journalists, news translators must work as if they were. We will see in more detail below what the process of news translation entails. At the moment, it will suffice to present it as an example of rewriting in the journalistic field, comparable to literary rewritings such as translations, anthologies, literary histories, biographies and book reviews, all of which, according to André Lefevere, entail similar processes of adaptation and manipulation of the original text (1992: 8).[3] Like literary rewritings, journalistic rewritings are the form in which news is made available to readers worldwide, although this fact is either generally hidden or taken for granted.

News translation challenges more traditional conceptions of the translator, whose role is in this context perceived in more active terms. José Manuel Vidal has put it as follows: 'El traductor de prensa es, quizás por la propia naturaleza del medio para el que traduce, un recreador, un escritor, delimitado por la idea que debe recrear y por el género periodístico en el que tiene que verter su traducción' (2005: 386) ('The news translator is, maybe because of the nature of the medium in which she writes, a re-creator, a writer, limited by the idea she has to re-create and by the journalistic genre in which her translation has to be done').

Multilingual journalists may not have specific training in translation as such, although they are often experts in news translation: able to produce fast and reliable translations on a wide range of subjects that are covered in the journalistic medium. Today, as in the early years, agency journalists are expected to be fluent in foreign languages. Moreover, both in AFP and Reuters one specific test for entry to work as news editor in a desk is the translation of a piece of news. The integration of translation in the production of news maximizes the efficiency of news organizations that have had, since their inception, to deal with linguistic diversity and to communicate information across linguistic borders. However, news organizations have also developed special structures that facilitate the flow of information and minimize the need for translation. The next section examines in more detail how global agencies deal with linguistic diversity and the role of translation at different stages of the production of news.

Dual agency networks: local and global journalists

News agencies have developed global networks which allow them to gather and distribute information worldwide with maximum effectiveness and at the greatest speed, while overcoming linguistic barriers. As we have seen in Chapter 3, the establishment of offices in the major European countries was achieved in a few decades after the creation of the news agencies and, in the course of the second half of the nineteenth century, the five continents were linked through telegraph lines and the establishment of permanent offices and agents. A pivotal element in the development of these networks is what could be analysed in terms of the news agencies' dual coverage structure. On the one hand, news agencies mobilize a core of foreign correspondents or global journalists worldwide. These highly mobile figures, who typically stay in foreign posts for periods of five years but also maintain close links with home, are employed by their national headquarters and tend to be British in the case of Reuters and French in the case of AFP. They produce news reports in the 'domestic' language of the global agency which appear untranslated in the main newswire (English in Reuters, French in AFP) and may also be translated for other newswires. On the other hand, local journalists are employed in the offices and bureaus that agencies maintain worldwide. These members of staff are not directly linked to the agency's headquarters and are in principle much less mobile (or only regionally so). They write news reports in their own language and translate news reports from the other wires so as to make them available to the local market. A typical agency bureau or regional office will thus employ two different kinds of journalists, global and local journalists, producing news in different languages for different newswires. For example, Reuters' bureau in Madrid employs Spanish journalists who write original reports in Spanish and translate reports written in English for the Spanish market, and international journalists who produce English-language reports about Spain for the English newswire.

This typical dual structure hugely reduces the need for translation, effectively minimizing the time it takes to circulate news worldwide in different languages and to different markets. It also implies a certain degree of decentralization, at least with reference to news content: the decision of what news reports are to be written or translated is taken by journalists who know the precise needs of their local or global markets at the local level. Reuters headquarters in London receives only news items in English from their international journalists for the English newswire. AFP Paris headquarters is differently organized and deals with a considerable amount of translation, which is typically done in the desks of the appropriate geographical regions. For example, the Latin American desk in Paris is responsible for translations into Spanish of news relating to Europe, the Middle East and Africa, while Spanish translations of news relating to the Americas are done in the regional desk in Montevideo.

In spite of news agencies having developed effective strategies and methods that hugely minimize the need for translation, the latter is still pivotal in all the stages involved in the production of news. Translation intervenes from the start in the process of news gathering, and is often the point of departure for international journalists who write about a foreign reality. The constant flow of international news around us hides the real difficulties that are part of reporting from remote areas, where the problem of not speaking the local language is added to those of access and background knowledge, while the issues involved in covering news about a foreign reality become in fact reduced to one of mere presence.[4]

Ulf Hannerz, who in the book *Transnational Connections* dedicates a chapter to the worldview of foreign correspondents, summarizes the working perspective of the global journalist succinctly as 'looking for trouble and the human interest story, in a pragmatic, instrumental, calculating way' (1996: 112), and gives as example the illustrative title of the autobiography of foreign correspondent Edward Behr: *Anyone Here Been Raped and Speaks English?* Hannerz compares the work of the correspondents, as key cultural intermediaries and specialized functionaries of the globalization of consciousness, to that of the anthropologists. One of the most interesting things in his chapter is that the author explicitly asks himself how correspondents deal with issues of understanding, with the problems of cultural translation, emphasizing the central importance of language. He arrives at the following conclusion: 'newspeople do not seem much given to deciphering foreign meanings at all. The working assumption, apparently, is that understanding is not a problem, things are what they seem to be' (1996: 120). Hannerz does not make explicit that this is not just the individual journalists' point of view, but rather the *habitus* or more endurable disposition of these actors in the journalistic field, and one of the central premises on which the circulation of global news is based: that we can all make sense of the images and the narratives that inform us almost instantly and continuously about developments in any part of the world, and that the knowledge derived from them effectively describes those realities.

As stated above, the figure of the translator is relatively rare in the news agencies, except with reference to a local journalist who provides linguistic and logistic help to an international journalist working in a foreign country the language of which he or she does not speak. If the foreign correspondent is the most visible face of international news organizations, often enjoying personal prestige and recognition, in some cases even considerable fame, the local translator can be considered the most humble and invisible among those directly involved in the production of global news.[5] The low status of this figure, generally known as the interpreter, is reflected in the way its task is often described and classified as part of a whole variety of local services, including drivers and other media assistants, that are needed by global journalists: 'news organizations have come to rely more than ever on locals for functions as basic as translation, landing interviews, finding electricity for laptops and satellite phones, and tracking down food in a desolate outpost' (Goldscheider, 2004: 36).

The news interpreter can thus be considered as the Other of the conference interpreter, who enjoys the highest prestige and remuneration in interpreting (Gile, 2004: 11). While both often work for international organizations and are important pieces in the infrastructure that allows the circulation of global information flows, the news interpreter is part of the place-bound local resources while both the conference interpreter and the international journalist belong to the highly mobile global cadres. The importance of the typically ignored figure of the interpreter is immense, as it acts as a sort of filter determining access for the international journalist. Some countries, for example China, have imposed at certain times global agencies' reliance on correspondents who do not know the language and used in this way local interpreters as an attempt to control the information that reaches international news markets. In addition, the low status of the news interpreter contrasts with the varied skills that are often required for the job. Thus, in the article referred to above, Eric Goldscheider quotes the deputy foreign editor of the *New York Times* stating that translation is just one measure of a good interpreter, who must also possess the qualities of a good journalist (background knowledge, ability to discern potential human-interest stories, eagerness in the pursuit of a story and so on). Often very exposed to dangers and even death because of their key mediating role, which cannot merely be understood as one of linguistic transfer but is necessarily one of cultural transfer, local interpreters are crucial in giving global news organizations access to their countries' otherwise unreachable reality.

The significance of the usually invisible news interpreter and their pivotal role in the circulation of international news are revealed in an episode narrated by Jean Huteau and Bernard Ullmann in their history of France-Presse, which is reproduced in full below:

9 septembre. La radio chinoise prévient qu'une 'importante annonce' sera faite à 16 heures. Dans le bureau de l'AFP, au huitième étage, à Qi Jia Yuan, autour du Grundig et du magnétophone, Biannic et les deux interprètes attendent.

Le correspondant de l'AFP a tenté de préparer M. Yuan, qui sait le français:
– Je ne voudrais pas m'avancer, mais je pense qu'il pourrait s'agir de la mort de votre grand dirigeant, le président Mao Tsé-toung.
– Oh non! C'est impossible!
– J'espère que non. Mais je le crains fort.

Alain Bouc, correspondant du *Monde*, passe par là, et Georges Biannic l'invite à rester à l'écoute de la radio.

A 4 heures de l'après-midi, le speaker entonne une longue litanie: 'Le Bureau politique, le Comité central, le Parti, le Conseil d'État, le Comité permanent de l'assemblée populaire nationale, les membres de l'Assemblée … '

Le temps s'arrête. La liste est interminable. La femme de ménage est entrée et se fige. Biannic jette un coup d'oeil au télétype de l'agence Chine nouvelle. Il diffuse aussi la liste. Lentement.

M. Yuan commence à comprendre et pâlit. Quand le mot fatal, dans le style noble qui convient à la mort d'un haut personnage, *shishi* … (a trépassé), est prononcé, il éclate en sanglots, de même que l'autre interprète et la femme de ménage. Au sein du concert de lamentations, Georges Biannic s'énerve: 'C'est bien ça? Mao est mort?'

L'interprète est incapable d'articuler un mot. Les secondes passent. Le scoop ne sera pas signé Biannic.

A l'AFP-Hong Kong, on ne pleure pas. Un rédacteur, David Lan, qui écoute aussi la radio, tape: 'Mao dead' en un temps record. L'AFP est la première, de peu, car toutes les agences étaient prévenues, mais c'est le fac-similé de sa dépêche que le *South China Morning Post* reproduit, le lendemain, en première page.

(1992: 367–68)

(The Chinese radio anticipates that an 'important announcement' will be made at 16 hours. At AFP's office on the 8th floor in Qi Jia Yuan, Biannic and the two interpreters are waiting by the transmitter and the tape recorder.

The AFP correspondent has tried to prepare Mr Yuan, who speaks French:
– I wouldn't want to anticipate events, but I think that this could be about the death of your great leader, President Mao Tse Tung.

– Oh no! This is impossible!

– I hope it isn't. But I fear it might be.

Alain Bouc, *Le Monde*'s correspondent, stops by and Georges Biannic invites him to stay and listen to the radio.

At 4 p.m., the speaker starts with a long litany: 'The Political Bureau, the Central Committee, the Party, the Council of State, the Permanent Committee of the National Popular Assembly, the members of the Assembly ... '

Time stops. The list never ends. The cleaning lady has entered and halts. Biannic glances at the teletype of the agency New China. It is also slowly printing the list.

Mr Yuan begins to understand and goes pale. When the fatal word is pronounced in the noble style that corresponds to the death of an important figure, *shishi* ... (has passed away), he bursts into tears, just like the other interpreter and the cleaning lady. In the midst of this concert of lamentations Georges Biannic asks nervously: 'Is that what it is? Is Mao dead?'

The interpreter is incapable of uttering a single word. The seconds go by. Biannic will not sign the scoop.

Nobody cries at AFP–Hong Kong's office. David Lan, an editor who is also listening to the radio, types: 'Mao dead' in a record time. AFP is the first, not by much, because all agencies had been warned, but it is the facsimile of its dispatch that the *South China Morning Post* reproduces, the day after, on its front page.)

In the above example, translation effectively delayed the circulation of a major item of breaking news for a few crucial seconds, and was the reason why AFP's correspondent in China missed an important scoop.[6] However, the normal workings of the news agencies ensure that translation does not hinder but rather facilitates the worldwide circulation of information to such an extent and with such a degree of effectiveness that translation itself becomes invisible and reaches the ideal of near-instantaneity that is a measure of the new demands placed on translation in the context of ever-increasing global information flows (see Chapter 2).

The nature of news translation

Approaches to news translation, a topic which has hardly been tackled in translation studies, are scarce. Moreover, many of the recently appeared contributions to the field consist of descriptive accounts from the point of view of experienced practitioners (García Suárez, 2005; Hursti, 2001; Tsai, 2005; Vidal, 2005). While these provide very valuable empirical accounts of translation practice in various news organizations and of the usual tasks and difficulties encountered by the translator of news, the need to systematically trace the theoretical implications from existing practice in very diverse organizations and the general principles that govern news translation remains. This section will delineate the main operations involved in the process of news translation, assess key concepts that have been proposed for describing this practice and critically discuss central issues in translation studies, such as equivalence and the notion of authorship that are problematized in news translation.

It could be argued that the main objective of news translation is the fast transmission of information in a clear way so that it can be communicated effectively to readers. Journalistic factors related to time, space and genre are as important as the linguistic and cultural aspects involved in the process of interlingual transfer. Bearing in mind the influence of the former, some major features which specifically characterize news translation and distinguish it from other forms have been pointed out:

1. The main objective of news translators is to transmit information.
2. News translators translate for a mass audience. Consequently, a clear and direct language needs to be used.
3. News translators translate for a specific geographical, temporal and cultural context. Their job is also conditioned by the medium in which they work.
4. News translators are subject to important limitations of time and space.
5. News translators are usually 'backtranslators' and proofreaders.

(Maria Josefina Tapia, quoted in Hernández Guerrero,
2005b: 157–58)

To these can be added a necessary versatility, which enables news translators to work on an immense variety of topics, from sports to economy. The link between these diverse subjects is the journalistic medium itself and the norms of genre and style to which all those working in the field are subjected.

In translating news, journalists must rewrite texts to make them suitable for their new context according to the rules and practices of the medium in which they work. News translation entails a considerable amount of transformation of the source text which results in the significantly different content of the target text. On the other hand, the process of news translation is not dissimilar from that of editing, through which news reports are checked, corrected, modified, polished up and prepared for publication. In this context, Karen Stetting proposed the concept of transediting as 'a new term for coping with the grey area between editing and translating' (1989: 371). While acknowledging that a certain amount of editing has always been part of the work of the translator, who needs to incorporate cultural and situational variations and who in many cases has to 'clean up' poor manuscripts, Stetting points to the fact that transediting is widely practised in certain types of translation to better suit the needs of the receivers: e.g. film and TV translation, TV interviews, written journalism, company and institutional brochures and PR material. Rather than adopting the somewhat artificial concept of transediting – the use of which would seem to imply the existence of another form of translating news – we will simply refer to news translation to point to this particular combination between editing and translating, and more specifically to the form that translation takes when it has become integrated in news production within the journalistic field.[7]

It is worthwhile looking in some detail at the most frequent modifications to which the source text can typically be subjected in the process of translation in order to illustrate the type of textual intervention required from the news translator:

- Change of title and lead: titles and leads (informative subtitles) are often substituted for new ones so as to better suit the needs of the target reader or the requirements of the target publication.
- Elimination of unnecessary information: information can become redundant either because it is already known by the target readers or because it becomes too detailed and specific for a reader who is geographically and culturally removed from the reality described.
- Addition of important background information: when the target readers change it becomes necessary to add background information that will not necessarily be known in the new context.
- Change in the order of paragraphs: the relevance of the information in a new context and the style of the publication might make it necessary to alter the order of paragraphs.
- Summarizing information: this method is often used to fit the source text into the space available and to reduce lengthy paragraphs which are no longer fully relevant to the target readers.

These alterations are usually justified by and respond to the two related criteria of news relevance and background knowledge of the target reader. The effect of this kind of intervention on the source text is to make its translated version more like an original, new text, specifically suited to the needs of the publication in which it appears and the readers to which it is targeted. As María José Hernández Guerrero remarks, the outcome of the process of news translation is the creation of a new text, destined to function as 'news' for a different public according to the textual conventions of another language (2005: 130–31).

The news translator has been presented above as a re-creator, a writer. It is clear that the kind of intervention demanded by news translation on the original text modifies the traditional role of the translator in relation to both the author and the source text. Translators' historical, cultural and socioeconomic dependence – their subordinate position in the cultural field – has been theorized in terms of their ingrained subservience 'to the client, to the public, to the author, to the text, to language itself' (Simeoni, 1998: 11–12). Stetting already pointed to the more interventionist role of the 'transeditor': 'if the translator decides to take on the more responsible role of "midwife" to see to it that the original intentions are reborn in a new and better shape in the target language, the translator turns into a "transeditor"' (1989: 376). The transeditor, challenging the secondary position traditionally attributed to the translator in relation to the writer, 'is also likely to feel that her work is more rewarding, if it is more independent and more on a par with that of the writer' (1989: 377).[8]

In the case of news translation which occupies us here, this role is none other than that of the journalist. Journalists who write original news reports are not any different from those who translate them. Moreover, the same person often combines both tasks indistinctively and translation is not felt to be something essentially dissimilar from other tasks involved in the production of news. Journalists tend to be initially surprised when they are asked about their role as news translators, because they do not see translation as a separate process from the edition of texts. It is only if they are led to do so by the researcher that they start reflecting on the specific nature of translation as such, and on the important part it plays in their everyday work and more generally in the production of news.

The journalist who writes a text does not possess a significantly different status from the journalist who translates it. Nor has the source text an essence that must be respected in the target text: it does not require that its form and content are preserved without significant alterations in translation, allowing the translator to adopt an interventionist role. The central importance of authorship, reflected in the sacrality of the original text, is a product of the autonomy of the literary field, and does not have an equivalent form in the highly heteronomous journalistic field. The news translator, unlike the literary translator, does not owe respect and faithfulness to the source text but is able to engage in a significantly different relationship with an often unsigned piece of news, the main purpose of which is to provide information of an event in a concise and clear way.

According to Pablo García Suárez, one of the main concerns of the news translator is the problem of objectivity rather than faithfulness to the source text, a feature that is particularly relevant and central in the translation of agency news, to which he refers:

> en el caso de un traductor de textos periodísticos, y en concreto de un traductor que trabaja en el seno de una agencia de noticias, lo que resulta en cambio característico es que la fidelidad al texto original está subordinada a la fidelidad a los hechos relatados, lo cual permite en ocasiones, y siempre que exista una clara justificación, introducir alteraciones en el sentido, intolerables para un traductor especializado en otros campos; es decir, le obliga a simultanear su labor traductora con la labor de redactor periodístico.
>
> (2005: 175–76)

(in the case of a news translator, and specifically of a translator who works in a news agency, what is characteristic is that faithfulness to the original text is subordinated to faithfulness to the narrated facts, which on some occasions and whenever there exists a clear justification allows for the introduction of alterations of meaning, which are intolerable to a translator specialized in other fields; that is to say, it obliges the translator to combine his translating task with the task of a journalistic editor.)

The issue of objectivity and of the particular style of agency news will be dealt with in the next section. However, the question of to whom or what must the news translator be faithful is a key one because it leads us to reflect on the nature of news translation and its differences or deviations from other forms of translation, which ultimately respond and can be traced back to concepts of equivalence. No matter how debated and ultimately questionable the notion of equivalence might be, it continues to be a central concept in translation studies, maybe because in a way it defines what translation itself is taken to be. Theories of dynamic or communicative equivalence, in which the key notion becomes 'equivalent effect' rather than identity, questioned and significantly enlarged early notions of (formal) equivalence that corresponded more to the concept of word-for-word translation. Nevertheless, even with broad and, according to some, essentially inaccurate and unmeasurable concepts such as Eugene Nida's dynamic equivalence, fundamental problems appear when we try to apply them to news translation.

In the article quoted above, Stetting had already identified this by pointing out that while equivalence is the central concern in the translation of cultural texts (by which she means high cultural or literary texts), the situation is different in the case of practical, everyday texts – defined as a wide range of non-fictional texts which include business materials and correspondence, advertising and journalistic texts – which are more open to 'interference' on the part of the translator (1989: 375).

Crucially, Anthony Pym has recently argued that

> The sheer quantities of weakly authored material now being translated have brought about significant differences in the professional tasks of many trained mediators, who are writing summaries, revising, providing linguistic consultation services, producing new texts for new readers, post-editing controlled translations, or managing language services. In such fields, the regulated replacement of natural-language strings often has a priority lower than effectiveness and timeliness. *Translations are thus to be assessed as new texts designed to serve new purposes, without any necessary constraint by equivalence.*
>
> (2004: 55, emphasis added)

Pym's analysis refers to the localization industry and his argument is that a localized text is not called to represent any previous text but it is rather part of a process of constant material distribution (2004: 5). This argument can similarly be applied to the translation (or localization) of news.

Equivalent effect is not preserved, for instance, when the news angle changes in translation, which is a perfectly normal operation in journalism if a new angle is justified according to the above-mentioned criteria of background knowledge and relevance. María José Hernández Guerrero gives an example of such a change in her study of the Spanish translation of a French report on the closure of part of the network of the Banque de France, which originally appeared in *Libération*. After commenting on the numerous changes, such as the transformation of title and lead and the elimination and addition of some information, she concludes: 'la función del original y traducción es la misma: informar, pero lo hacen desde una perspectiva distinta; mientras el original profundiza más en la postura de los sindicatos franceses, la traducción española abunda más en la explicación del porqué de las medidas adoptadas en Francia' (2005: 100) ('the function of the original and the translation is the same: to inform, but they do it from a different perspective; while the original deals in more depth with the position of the French trade unions, the Spanish translation centres on explaining the reason for the measures taken in France'). This change of news angle is not only usual in translations of news reports from different organizations, but is also frequent within the same organization as in the case of news agencies, especially in a type of translation involving the combined use of different source texts with the purpose to rework them and summarize them in a single target text.

The example mentioned above would, following an idea of equivalence, not be considered a translation. Yet, it is precisely the change of angle that makes it a successful translation, able to function as news for the Spanish public. In other words, it is effective as news not because it has reached equivalent effect – itself a superfluous objective because in Spain the closure of the French Central Bank does not have the same relevance it has in France – but because it is able to communicate effectively across linguistic, cultural and geographical boundaries, and inform new readers precisely of those aspects on which they need to be informed.

The translation of agency news

News agencies fulfil a key role in the circulation of global news. As we have seen, a very large amount of their output consists of translations, which they make available to clients in different news markets in various languages. Translation in news agencies is thus, in quantitative terms, of central importance. But it is also of special significance because news agencies are in many cases the first to approach and describe new realities, creating ways of addressing them and introducing new vocabulary to represent them, thus exerting a palpable influence upon other news organizations. Pablo García Suárez has expressed this important point as follows:

> Las agencias de noticias pueden considerarse la 'primera línea de combate' en la traducción de términos que designan realidades nuevas. Su carácter

de fuente de la prensa escrita, radio y televisión, hace que el redactor de una agencia, y sobre todo el traductor de sus noticias, sea casi el primero en tener que resolver los problemas asociados a la asimilación de realidades nuevas por una determinada cultura. Por lo tanto su responsabilidad es grande, ya que los nuevos términos pasarán de las agencias de noticias a la prensa, y de ella a menudo tomarán las soluciones aportadas los traductores técnicos...

(García Suárez, 2005: 187)

(News agencies can be considered the 'first line of combat' in the translation of terms designating new realities. Because of their character as sources for the written press, radio and television, news agency editors, and especially news translators, are almost the first to have to solve the problems associated with the assimilation of new realities in a certain culture. Therefore, their responsibility is high, as new terms will be transmitted from the news agencies to the press, and technical translators will often adopt the solutions given by the latter...)

A general characterization of the process of news translation has been offered in the previous section. This section will devote closer attention to translation practices in news agencies, describing central aspects of agency work and the nature of agency news and examining in detail how news agencies deal with questions concerning translation. As indicated above, translation is not separate from other operations and practices involved in the production of news; a consideration of translation practices in news agencies will thus imply a more general examination of the main processes involved in news production in these organizations.

Journalistic texts can be broadly divided into informative genres (the typical news report, containing factual descriptions of events), interpretative genres (such as reportage, in which information is selected, interpreted and narrated by the journalist) and argumentative genres (in which the author's style, who is often not a journalist, prevails, such as the opinion article or the column). Different journalistic genres generate specific translation rules and strategies. While informative genres – in which the author's personal style is reduced to the minimum – typically offer the maximum space for intervention and alteration of the original text, the translation of argumentative genres, which is close to literary translation, implies a much smaller space for alteration and, at the same time, a high degree of subordination to the author's style. News agencies produce mostly texts of the first type – informative genres – explicitly conceived as narration of fact devoid of subjective commentary. Translation of agency news will consequently be generally characterized by a relatively high degree of transformation of the source text.

Two fundamental principles regulate the production of agency news: speed and hierarchy. News agencies have devised their own formula to inform about developments as they take place while discriminating between their degree of importance, a fundamental thing given the amount of events covered and the requirement that clients be able to discern important information that concerns them immediately. Typically, an event classified as priority is first announced in just a few words, which will soon be followed by longer informative notes. There is a strict time limit (usually no longer than ten minutes) set for writing through important information – highest priority items such as the alert or the news bulletin and second priority items such as the newsbreak or urgent – in the form of updates, which add new developments, context, interpretation and background. Updates are numbered and regularly substituted by new ones that follow the development of events. They are all factual descriptions of news events containing a complete story, which can be printed in the newspapers as it comes. Word limits are always very strict, from only a few words in the case of information of the highest priority to usually about 400 to 600 words for updates.

A basic tool of agency work which is ideally suited to the fundamental principles of speed and hierarchy is the method of the inverted pyramid, in which the elements of the story are written up in declining order of importance, so that essential information comes first and is developed in subsequent paragraphs, which add background and secondary information. An agency dispatch is written in such a way that it can be cut by the client from the bottom up, without it being necessary to alter its contents in any other way. It thus facilitates not only a quick grasp of the most relevant information, but also the personalized use of subscribing organizations.

Strict rules also apply with respect to style, which is kept simple and clear. Conciseness is emphasized in order to maximize informative content. Sentences and paragraphs must be short and economical, the use of active rather than passive verbs is preferred and the presence of adjectives limited. These stylistic rules are also ideally suited to the traditional agency values of objectivity and neutrality, an expression of the fact that news is a marketable commodity to be sold to a whole range of different media. This not only has a determining influence on translation but also facilitates it, by homogenizing criteria and subjecting the translator's creativity to strict norms. In addition, news agencies have harmonized structures, classificatory conventions and presentation criteria across all languages and desks, which also contributes to the process of translation.[9] In short, the author or translator's individual style is sacrificed or neutralized in favour of a unified style, usually embodied in the organization's style book (García Suárez, 2005: 177; Hernández Guerrero, 2005b: 159).

As has been argued above, if the news translator does not owe the same kind of subservience to the author as the literary translator, it is because in journalism the status and role of the author are fundamentally different than in the literary field. In most news organizations, the norm is that several journalists are involved in the production of a story, which must always be subjected to the finishing touches of an editor. Authorship is thus no longer strictly individual, a fact that is related to the potential legal implications of publishing certain information and also to the need to ensure the correct application of the news organization's norms. In news agencies, this principle of collective authorship is strongly reinforced so that 'everyone who touches a story is responsible and accountable for its contents' (*A Handbook of Reuters Journalism*, p. 61). Texts are not allowed to circulate on the newswire if they are not previously checked by an editor, who assumes co-responsibility for both content (sources, accuracy, background) and style. The same applies to translated dispatches, which are always read by a second pair of eyes. This principle of collective authorship is reflected in the multiple signature which figures at the end of all news dispatches, consisting of the initials of the journalist who wrote the report, the journalist who edited it and, in the case of translated reports, also the initials of the translator and the editor who checked the translation.

Agency style manuals are useful codes specifying and regulating the most important operations for the production of news. In addition to covering the journalistic tasks of sourcing, reporting and writing basics, journalistic values, news structure and style, they contain numerous remarks on the correct use of language, sometimes full style guides addressing potentially problematic words as well as specific genres with a high level of semantic specialization, such as sports. Agency manuals do not include full sections on the translation of news, and only a few remarks specifically dealing with translation.[10] However, this should not be taken as a sign of the secondary importance of translation in news agencies, but rather as an indication of the extent to which translation has been integrated with other processes involved in the production of news. Thus, *AFP's Manual of the Spanish Service* identifies translation as one of the main tasks of the desk: translation appears in the second place, listed directly after the task of selecting and sending texts to the newswire (p. 71). Reuters' *Handbook* omits any reference of this kind, and does not mention translation as one of the functions of the desk.[11] However, the central place that translation occupies in news production is made explicit in the following reference to how news reports should be written: 'The basic spot news story is the mainstay of the Reuters file. Write it quickly, clearly and simply. Say what happened and why we are reporting it, *in language that is easy to translate*' (p. 56, emphasis added).

Translation in news agencies follows the general reporting and writing rules identified above with reference to speed, clarity and style. Generally, agency manuals do not deal separately with the translation of news.[12] However, they do regulate certain specific cases and situations explicitly involving translation. Moreover, these regulations tend to be similar in different organizations. What follows is an analysis of these specific stipulations concerning translation in news agencies. First, translation must never delay the circulation of important information, especially in certain cases when it is possible to prepare news reports in advance. When news pieces can be written ahead of anticipated or set events ('curtainraisers'), the reporter must file them with the time required by the linguistic services in order to translate them (AFP, p. 37). Similarly, embargoed material (which cannot be either transmitted or published until the time designated for its official release) needs to be sent to the appropriate desks so that it can also be translated into other languages in advance (AFP, p. 72). The transmission of a Reuters' video script should never be delayed by the translation or transcription of a quote, and it is possible to send the full script when it is complete after the images have already reached the clients (Reuters, p. 98).

The nature of agency work places a fundamental importance on direct sources. Moreover, news agencies also insist on quoting these sources whenever possible, rather than paraphrasing them. Special care is taken in the translation of these quotes, and the desk can ask a reporter or producer to obtain original quotes when they are in a different language to that of the report (AFP, p. 69). Reuters' *Handbook* (p. 11) gives specific instructions for the translation of quotes:

> When translating quotes from one language into another, we should do so in an idiomatic way rather than with pedantic literalness. Care must be taken to ensure that the tone of the translation is equivalent to the tone of the original. Beware of translating quotes in newspaper pickups back into the original language of the source. If a French politician gives an interview to an American newspaper, it is almost certain that the translation back into French will be wrong and in some cases the quote could be very different. In such cases, the fewer quotes and the more reported speech, the better.

Translation of official statements and documents is also an important service provided by the news agencies. In these cases, it is always necessary to indicate the language of the original and the source of the translation (whether it is official or an agency translation) (AFP, p. 34; Reuters, p. 58).

A final remark must be made in this section on translation in news agencies to the growing, almost absolute dominance of English when dealing with images (in both photographic and video services). AFP is currently in the process of implementing a new policy through which, no matter where they are produced and treated, photographs are always to be described by English-language captions. Reuters' video news is accompanied by a script in English, which also requires the translation of all quotes into this language (although a German video service also exists specifically destined to that market). With respect to the circulation of images, global monolinguism prevails, and translation is undertaken by the subscribing news organizations themselves, rather than by the news agencies.

Conclusion

During the second half of the twentieth century, a growing mediatization of world events led to the emergence of the global media events that we have become so familiar with today. The news agencies specialized since the nineteenth century in the fast and reliable coverage of events worldwide, and their expanding infrastructures were in many ways the expression of the rising demand for world news. Increasing media interest in the coverage of the most diverse topics from wars to sport is for example revealed in the operations that AFP set in motion for the Olympic Games. During the London 1948 Olympics, it only mobilized four journalists and the amount of information circulated on classifications and results was very limited. However, by the Melbourne Olympics (1956), AFP's service had become exhaustive and circulated, in addition to the full results of all competitions, interviews, features and special reports destined to specific regions or countries. Fifty-nine countries had participated in the London Olympics; twenty years later, 115 countries participated in the Mexico games, for which AFP mobilized 30 journalists (Huteau and Ullmann, 1992: 272–73). This not only responds to AFP's effort to establish its sports service to the highest standards, but also and especially to the increasing media importance of international sports events. A similar development took place after 1958 with information concerning the Vatican, which experienced a true media explosion in a few years and became consolidated, with Pope John Paul II, as affecting not only the Catholic countries but the whole planet (Huteau and Ullmann, 1992: 364).

Today, the media impact of 9/11 epitomizes the new significance of world events taking place in front of a global public in real time. The importance of this kind of global media event is certainly undeniable; however, it would be wrong to assume the instantaneous intelligibility of the same messages worldwide, even when it is continuously being asserted by the endless repetition of powerful television images of disasters, acts of terror and war. Most information about world events needs to be tailored to specific publics, and the way in which narratives of global media events are constructed for local audiences is mediated by translation. Translation fulfils a pivotal role in the circulation of global news by producing significantly different local versions of international events. As we have seen, in part it is the global media organizations themselves (such as the news agencies or the channels of continuous information) that are responsible for the translation of news. In other cases, local media organizations transform the messages circulated globally to cater for their audiences. Global and local media organizations rewrite texts so that we are (but in fact we are not) watching, listening to and reading about the same events, and thus a multitude of local versions and narratives of global events exists.

If the first point of this conclusion asserts and emphasizes the ubiquity of translation in the circulation of global news and its pivotal role in rewriting texts for local audiences, the second refers to the type of intervention that it effects on the news text. As in the critical commentary of (translated) literature (Venuti, 1995) or in travel writing (Cronin, 2000), the role of translation in the production of news is invisible. Moreover, it could be argued that news translation is doubly invisible, not just because of the need to adopt a domesticating strategy that values fluency and hides its very intervention, but also because of the fact that translation has been successfully integrated within journalism. News translation is subject to the norms that regulate news production more generally, and falls within the range of expertise of those trained and specialized in the production of news: the journalists. Like other significant social groups such as anthropologists, missionaries, tourists or translators engaged in travel and intercultural communication, journalists are actors of the contact zone. Journalists – as news translators – fulfil the important task of rewriting news texts so as to make them suitable for different linguistic, cultural and geographical contexts. Moreover, their role and type of intervention takes on a paradoxical form. On the one hand, the informative and communicative purposes of the journalistic text, the functional use of language, simple vocabulary and short sentences, facilitate the task of translation and subject it, at the same time, to a very strict normative context which greatly limits the space for individual creativity and originality. On the other, through translation, the journalist transforms the original text in important ways, in a context in which faithfulness is due more to the narrated events than to the source text. A theorization of this type of textual intervention and of the until recently neglected area of news translation will lead the discipline of translation studies in new and interesting directions.

5 Journalism and translation
Practices, strategies and values in the news agencies

The previous chapter discussed the nature and significance of news translation and analysed the main mechanisms through which it has been successfully integrated in the production of news. This chapter deals with translation in news agencies in more detail, examining existing practices in different organizations more closely and devoting attention to specific strategies and values and to the views and conceptions of the journalists themselves.

The main basis of this chapter is fieldwork conducted at AFP and IPS' regional headquarters for Latin America in Montevideo, where a period of two weeks of ethnographic observation was spent in June 2004. During this period journalists and translators working at both regional desks were interviewed. At IPS, six journalists were interviewed, including the regional editor for Latin America, a senior member of the organization with a managerial role, two translators-editors and two editors. Eleven journalists were interviewed at AFP, including its regional editor, the desk's chief editor and another nine editors. In addition, several online questionnaires were sent to various journalists at AFP, IPS and Reuters, and a fieldtrip to Reuters' headquarters in London took place in May 2004.

In what follows the role of news agencies' regional centres is discussed, a dominant and an alternative model for translation presented, and actual practices at IPS and AFP compared, making ample use of the material obtained through extensive semi-structured interviews maintained with journalists working at both organizations.

News agencies' regional centres: mediating between the local and the global

News agencies have achieved maximum efficiency in the dissemination of news worldwide through the coordination between local offices, in which news reports are written, and regional or global centres where information is filtered, translated and edited. As we saw in Chapter 3, in the past decades there has been a progressive trend towards decentralization, so that today important regional centres exist and operate with a relative degree of autonomy from the organization's global headquarters. News reports are written at the local level and then transmitted to the appropriate regional centre, which houses the desk, where information is processed and sent to the newswire. At the same time, the regional headquarters mediate with the local offices by coordinating coverage and commissioning specific pieces, and by bringing together the outputs from the different offices in the region. Thus, only the regional centre has a view on the global coverage of events, which is lost at the local level. The type of job journalists perform at regional centres also differs significantly from that of their counterparts at the local level. While journalists in local offices write original news pieces, editors working in the desk are responsible only for the processing of information which has been written by someone else: editing or translating reports from other linguistic services in order to validate them for a particular newswire. Seldom do they fulfil the function of primary news gathering, although they can also be given assignments to cover specific events, often involving international travel within the region.

With corporate headquarters in London, Reuters is organized into three regions: Europe, Middle East and Africa (headquarters in Collonge-Bellerive, Switzerland), the Americas (headquarters New York) and Asia/Pacific (headquarters Singapore). Agence France-Presse has its world headquarters in Paris and is organized into five regions: North America (headquarters in Washington), Latin America (headquarters in Montevideo), Asia/Pacific (headquarters Hong Kong), Europe/Africa (headquarters Paris), Middle East (headquarters Nicosia). Inter Press Service, with headquarters in Rome, is organized into five regions: Africa (headquarters Johannesburg), Asia/Pacific (headquarters Bangkok), Europe/Mediterranean (headquarters Berlin), Latin America (headquarters Montevideo) and North America and Caribbean. Geographical location reflects news agencies' historical presence in certain regions as well as the lesser news significance of areas like Africa, where only IPS maintains a regional centre.

Housing Inter Press Service's regional offices for the Americas and AFP's regional headquarters for Latin America, Montevideo is a continental capital of agency journalism. Previously located in Costa Rica, IPS established its offices in the city in 1994. Montevideo is also its world centre for translation. The high educational level of the general population – as well as low salaries – might be pointed at as reasons for this choice, which significantly coincides with AFP's. More generally, IPS' prominence in Latin America has a long history. IPS emerged in the mid-1960s as an exchange agency between Latin America and Europe, in the context in which the economic, political and communications systems were profoundly questioned and alternatives for a new world information and communication order were being actively sought. For many years, Spanish remained its main language, and its principal client base was found in Latin American media outlets. The agency still retains its largest media client base in the region, although in the past decades significant changes have taken place transforming the nature of the organization in important ways. On the one hand, IPS has gradually ceased competing with other news agencies in the region, specializing in a different kind of news product offering in-depth coverage and analysis, and communicating directly to the public through the internet. Although it possesses a significant presence in some media outlets in the south, it has also developed an important client base in international, regional or local NGOs and is also addressed to civil society. On the other hand, since the 1970s with the coverage of UN summits and conferences, English has progressively gained importance in the organization.

Montevideo's regional desk is in charge of coordinating Latin American coverage and of the edition and translation of the global services. It has an editorial staff of seven, including a regional editor, two translators-editors from Spanish into English, two translators-editors from English into Spanish, and four Spanish-language editors. Although their title is formally different, it must be noted that editors ordinarily translate, and their everyday tasks are not substantially different than those of the translators-editors. While translators-editors have a translation or academic background, all of the editors have wide journalistic experience of working in various media. IPS' global services' daily output is about thirty analytical features (of about 1,200 words) per day, about 40 per cent of which are in Spanish. This includes a number of translations: five or six of the news features published in English are translations from Spanish-language texts, and four or five of the Spanish articles are translated from English. In addition, selections from the global services are translated locally from English or Spanish into fourteen other languages. Other journalistic products at the Latin American desk include a service of shorter notes (*Breves*), articles kept to a length of 2,000–3,000 bytes, which has recently been introduced in Spanish, more in news-agency style of breaking news coverage.

AFP's prominent presence in the Latin American news market goes back to the partition of the world between the leading news agencies in the nineteenth century. The Spanish service, which by the 1980s transmitted about 20,000 words daily, was traditionally handled from the Paris headquarters. Initial decentralization started at that time, but the Latin American desk remained in Paris until the creation of the regional centre in Montevideo in 1997. Today, this centre is responsible for coordinating the output of twenty-one Latin American offices and for processing information related to the Americas in Spanish, while Spanish-language information relating to Europe, Asia and Africa is handled in Paris. Montevideo also produces *¡AFP Ya!*, its internet newspaper in Spanish destined to the Latin American news market (a different one called *¡Madrid!* is produced in Spain). According to a news editor, about 70–80 per cent of the material that reaches the desk is in Spanish and translations account for about 30 per cent. This relationship is inverted at the Latin American desk in Paris, where only 20–30 per cent of the processed information is in Spanish and most of the output in that language is derived from translations. Spanish is AFP's third language in importance, after French and English, of global distribution, disseminated in the Americas and Europe, and the agency maintains reporters in the three languages in a growing number of key offices. Other linguistic services offered by the agency, such as the German newswire, which is circumscribed to the German-speaking countries (mainly Austria and Germany), are of a more local character. The total output of the Spanish service is calculated at about 230,000 words each day (of a global output which reaches 600,000 words).

Montevideo's desk is staffed by a chief regional editor, a desk chief, fifteen Spanish-language editors and two French-language editors. In addition, there are six editors dedicated to sports and a photographic service. At the desk, texts produced in Spanish at the local offices of the region are edited, and English- and French-language texts dealing with the Americas are translated into Spanish. In addition, the two French-language regional editors translate Spanish-language reports into French and are also frequently sent to cover events in the region to supplement coverage (in French) destined for European audiences. The desk functions continuously from 7 a.m. to 3 a.m. and is thus only left unstaffed for four hours at night, during which the international office based in Paris takes over. It has a daily production of about 500 texts, which can range from one-line bulletins of urgent information to the usual notes and updates, which are approximately 400 to 600 words in length. According to a news editor, about 40 per cent of these texts deal with political issues, 15–20 per cent with economic issues, a similar amount with society issues and 15 per cent with sports. While most of the editors working at the desk deal with general information (except sports, for which there is a special service), there is also some degree of specialization and two journalists are primarily in charge of society themes, while another two are responsible for economic information.

One of the functions of regional centres, both at IPS and at AFP, is the mediation between news gathering at the local level and the production of a coherent and comprehensive global information service. Both centres coordinate coverage of the local offices of the region, while communicating with other regions. In IPS, issues of coverage and editorial lines are discussed at a weekly virtual meeting in which the editor-in-chief (based in Rome), the coordinator of translation from Spanish into English and the editors of the five regions participate. In AFP, every morning (10.00 a.m. in Montevideo; 2.00 GMT) a telephone conference takes place in which the world editor-in-chief and the chief editors of the five regions participate. In it, each region's agenda (previously put together by the chief regional editor in consultation with the local offices of the region) is discussed and the main themes of the day, as well as the news angle through which they are to be approached, approved. This coordination between the local, the regional and the global levels responds to a basic operational dynamic which structures world coverage according to previsions – although the capacity to respond immediately to unexpected events is also essential. Working to daily and weekly previsions is not only an operational feature of news agencies, but is itself one of the products they offer to their clients (AFP circulates listings of the main themes of the day, a product which is called 'Previsions', at 17.00 hours GMT), allowing editors of newspapers and broadcast media to clearly follow the hierarchy of information established in the newswire, to have a general view of events and to programme their daily coverage.

Daily reality in the news agencies is inseparable from the wider journalistic field of which they are part. At AFP's headquarters, located in a modern building with magnificent views from the seventh floor of Plaza Independencia, at the heart of the city, journalists read the local and international press, and CNN or TVE (Spanish International Channel) are often on. The presence of the continuous information channels is significant and reveals the changed status of the news agency, today no longer the exclusive source of international breaking news. The alarms of urgent information entering the newswire regularly go off, often provoking exclamations of surprise and further acceleration of the already frantic pace of work. Only a few streets away, at IPS' headquarters, the chosen information channels tend to be BBC radio and BBC World, there is no sound of alarms and the general pace of work, although still responding to the need for the timely circulation of information, is very different.

Journalists do not only look at the press to find out about events, or not primarily for this purpose – after all, they have the most comprehensive source of breaking news in their own newswire. Rather, they are primarily seeking to follow the interests and news angles of the media and the trajectory of their own notes. Checking whether and where their news articles have been picked up and published by subscribing media – indeed, whether they have been able to beat the competition from other agencies on one particular subject – is not only part of the job of individual journalists in this highly competitive field, but is also taken up at the highest organizational level. It is the task of every news agency to scan the local press and to measure its impact in terms of number of news dispatches appeared in the media while contrasting it with the impact of other agencies present in the field, data which is moreover often treated with high levels of secrecy and zealously kept from outsiders.

However, a cursory glance at the local press for a few days can reveal an approximate map of impact for research purposes. A quick examination of the international pages of Montevideo's most significant newspapers (*El País*, *El Observador* and *La República*) shows their strong dependency on the news agencies for international news, a characteristic feature of media in poorer countries which has already been pointed out in Chapter 3. Newspapers, often pressed for economic resources, find it impossible to maintain their own international correspondents, except in some cases in neighbouring Argentina or Brazil. The predominance of AFP, the Italian ANSA, as well as of the Spanish EFE and of Associated Press and the almost total absence of Reuters, can also be easily discerned. In this respect, AFP's regional editor for Latin America states:

Our main competitors in the region are AP and EFE; Reuters would come after that. With relation to AP I don't really know if we have a linguistic difference, but our Spanish service is put together by Latin Americans ... If there really is a difference it is a difference of contents, of focus, of ways of covering information, of different angles; our point of view is not necessarily North American ... On the other hand, there is a big difference with respect to EFE's offer which, of course, has a Spanish-language service more in Spanish from Spain. And in this sense I think that the service we offer is more eclectic ... We try to have very varied staff ... we have people from everywhere ... We try to have an eclectic Spanish that does not represent anybody in particular and that is a language of communication for all.

In spite of having ceased to compete with the other news agencies on equal terms, IPS still retains a significant presence in local media, and its articles are often published by subscribing newspaper *La República*. Further, IPS has no longer any significant competitors offering an alternative news product, as many small regional agencies have disappeared or become much smaller in recent decades.

AFP and IPS: the dominant and the alternative model of translation

As we have already pointed out, the regions function with a relative degree of autonomy so that coverage is determined at the regional or local level by journalists who are aware of the specific needs of that market. This is also the case for translation. IPS' global coverage is coordinated with the regions, but semi-autonomous local branches of the organization are responsible for the further translation of the global services and for the elaboration and distribution of a local service. Moreover, in the case of European local agencies, they are not subsidized by IPS, because resources are destined for the South, and have to find their own means of subsistence through local sales and funding.

In AFP's regional headquarters journalists translate reports from the French and English newswires for the Spanish wire, and a French-language version of Spanish-language news about Latin America is also produced. As we have seen, agencies' dual (and in this case sometimes tertiary) structures ensure that important events are covered in parallel for the different linguistic services. This means that events of global significance are reported at the same time in Spanish, in English and in French, through articles that incorporate regional nuances and are thus designed for their specific audiences from the start. Nevertheless, an important part of work at the desk (about one-third) is dedicated to translation. In IPS' Montevideo office, its world centre for translation, translations from and to English and Spanish, the two global languages of the organization, are produced. Translation is thus an integral part of journalistic work at both regional offices, where news reports are processed, which will further be translated into other languages at the local level.

While translation is important in the production of news in the two news agencies, practices significantly differ. Leading global news agencies have adapted their linguistic policy to the needs of their main news markets and, as a consequence, embraced production in only a few major languages. The advantage of regional centres such as those located in Montevideo is that journalists who know the needs of the local markets and have at the same time a global view on the agency's coverage of events are in charge of selecting and translating the information.

As we have seen, editors working at AFP's regional desk come from a wide variety of countries in Latin America, although journalists from the River Plate region predominate. Geographical diversity is an explicit recruiting policy not just because of the need to produce a newswire in a standard Spanish that can be understood and used in the whole region, but also because of the knowledge that these journalists have of different countries in the region and their ability to discern the significance of local events in those countries. Working languages of AFP editors at Montevideo are Spanish, English and French and a command of the three is now a customary requirement for entry (although many journalists working at the desk speak other languages as well). In this respect, AFP significantly differs from the Anglo-American news agencies, where working languages are usually two, English and a local language. All editors have a journalistic background with ample experience in different media, especially newspapers, and many have been agency reporters for a number of years before being transferred to the desk. In addition, most editors, and especially all the younger ones, have degrees in media and communications.

IPS' politics with regard to language stems from its aim of global inclusion. IPS' objective of 'balanced representation of ethnic diversity and geographical distribution' has direct implications for its linguistic politics, in particular the promotion of equality between languages. The organization thus encourages communication between minority languages, both European and non-European, and translation into the highest amount of languages possible so as to achieve a presence in local media. While, for operative purposes, global services are limited to two languages, English and Spanish, often very good local selections in minority languages exist. IPS' had the first international news service in Swahili in the 1980s and today is the only agency producing in languages such as Nepali or Thai. IPS' central concern is not formulated in terms of maintaining a presence in the main news markets, but in terms of reaching local publics, especially in the Third World, and this is the main reason why the organization embraces languages that have hitherto had little significance in the production of news. IPS' editor-in-chief, Miren Gutiérrez, explains the nature of the agency's approach to language and translation as follows:

> IPS has traditionally been an English–Spanish service. But our main aim is to have local impact. I'll give you an example of how important

translations can be, especially in the context of peacemaking. In the Sri Lankan peace process, IPS' news and analysis was made available simultaneously in Tamil, Sinhala and English. Whilst this met with initial resistance (to the extent that contracted translators at first refused to translate material not perceived as originating from 'their' side), once this was overcome there was explicit recognition of the value of a common platform of communication. We are trying to launch a service in Arabic and Hebrew with the same approach.

The organization's editorial line has also given origin to a very different type of agency text: longer features or analyses dealing with the major global themes that are prioritized by the agency from news angles that privilege the perspectives of civil society and the South. IPS' features must contain at least two sources (one of which must be from non-official circles) and need to adopt an in-depth perspective in order to explain the context in which events occur. Articles are also always signed by the reporters who write them. In contrast with other agencies, which offer subscribing media the freedom to alter contents in any way deemed appropriate, and even not to credit the agency, IPS' features cannot be changed and must be reproduced in full. A notion of inverted pyramid structure is retained, but it is applied more loosely than in the other news agencies.

These alternative politics of language have also led the organization to adopt a different model of translation which can be contrasted to the dominant model, represented by major news agencies such as Reuters and AFP. As we have seen, in the dominant model, translation is fully incorporated into the production of news. This means that news texts are translated by journalists who do not normally have any specific training as translators. Neither Reuters nor France-Presse employ any translators. Thus, AFP's chief of the Spanish desk states:

> I don't want to use the word translator, because none of the journalists working for us are translators: they are editors. By necessity they must rework ... choose any word you like: rework, edit, modify. The one I prefer is to edit. There are no translators working here. We select journalists and not translators, journalists who must at least know two languages in addition to Spanish and journalists who have previous experience, if possible in various media, agencies, radio, newspapers.

However, the importance of translation for news production at these agencies is paramount, as can be illustrated by the fact that an entry test for journalists in the regional bureaus of both AFP and Reuters is a test in news translation. The job title of journalists working at the desk is news editor, although their main activity is both translation and edition of texts. In this dominant model, only people who possess a journalistic training are seen to have the specific skills needed to produce the sort of translations required, which always include a degree of transformation and rewriting to suit the needs of specific audiences.

The alternative model of translation at IPS bears significant differences with the prevalent model at the big news agencies and has given origin in particular to the hybrid figure of the translator-editor. At Montevideo's Spanish desk, we find Spanish-language editors with a journalistic background whose task is not only editing but also translation of texts. However, IPS employs in addition professional translators who have the title of translators-editors, with a translation or academic background. Thus, at the IPS' desk, journalists and translators work side by side and undertake similar tasks of edition and translation of texts. Knowledge of both English and Spanish is required.

Although the work IPS' translators and editors do is similar to that of the journalists in the dominant model, in that it includes the same degree of transformation of the news text, the conditions in which they do it vary. IPS' news reports are longer and of a more analytical nature, and there is usually more time to translate them (a translation can take up to two hours, while in AFP it rarely takes longer than thirty minutes). The daily quota of a translator or editor at IPS' is five texts, while at AFP individual journalists process up to thirty to forty texts of all sizes daily, ranging from a couple of lines of urgent information, which must be translated instantly, to 600-word updates. While texts to be translated or edited in the dominant model are distributed by the desk chief, the work at IPS tends to be more autonomous, and translators and editors often choose the texts to be translated themselves. In the minority model the translator is individually responsible for the final text (except editors of recent incorporation, whose texts are checked and edited by a more experienced colleague), while in the dominant model all translations are edited by a second person. A common feature in both models is that translations are not signed and do not appear explicitly as such, although texts are marked with the initials of the reporter, the editor, the translator and, in the case of AFP, the person who has edited the translation, which identifies the person responsible for each process within the agency.

In addition to the news editors who work at the desk, IPS employs four translators-editors: two in the Spanish to English service and two in the English to Spanish service. Typically, they started working as translators and have gradually acquired a more journalistic function, which makes their role hardly distinguishable from that of the other news editors. Thus, of the two translators interviewed during fieldwork, one acts as coordinator of translations from Spanish into English and as such deals with questions of coverage and angle and participates in editorial meetings, while the other has recently started writing her own articles for a Spanish-language publication linked to the agency. Both translators also regularly edit texts for their respective linguistic services. While the first, who has an academic background, when asked whether she sees herself as a translator or as a journalist, identifies herself explicitly as a translator, the second – who has a translation background and regularly works as freelance translator – has a more mixed opinion of her role and position:

> I am maybe both. I studied to be a translator and when I started to work here it was as a translator. But this job involves as much journalism as translation. I learned with time, absorbing those themes. And currently I think that indeed I am partly a journalist. I have even started collaborating with a publication, *Tierramérica*, in which I write articles. I have also been sent to cover conferences on sustainable development ... If you are not partly a journalist, you cannot really do this job.

Generally, it is very difficult to conceptualize a difference between editors from translation and from journalistic backgrounds because, in order to work as news translators, translators have in fact to become journalists. They must select, edit and prioritize texts and information following prevailing journalistic criteria to ensure maximum impact. What characterizes a journalist who translates news is often a background in news production, a previous experience as reporter, which is usually maintained in news agencies such as AFP, where editors at the desk can be sent as correspondents to cover special events taking place in any country of the region. The fact that part of the journalist's job is to investigate and add new data when needed, which is vital in translating news for different audiences, is seen to distinguish it from the translator, who is viewed as a more passive conveyer of information which is already there. Journalists also often explicitly point at their first-hand experience of news reporting in different contexts as being a valuable asset when translating news, not just because of better knowledge of the kind of texts to be translated and the realities described, but also because they have a more sympathetic attitude towards the producer, and often consult with the person who has originally written the news. On the other hand, as will be analysed in more detail below, journalists point out that their first priority is always comprehension, rather than literality and faithfulness, and that they tend to be less fussy about correctness.

However, IPS' alternative model of translation does promote a more visible and more prominent role of this activity by recognizing, distinguishing and thus ultimately empowering translators as such – rather than only indirectly as journalists. Moreover, the organization has also allowed translators to take a more interventionist role in editorial matters, expressed in the creation of the figure of coordinator of translations, who has taken an unusually proactive role and currently participates in the agency's editorial meetings, together with the regional editors and the editor-in-chief. However, and from another point of view, it has been pointed out that the fact that translation is not wholly based upon the work of journalists who speak several languages as in the dominant model but on the work of translators who are not necessarily journalists can take away some of the journalistic flavour to their texts. What this 'journalistic flavour' or rhythm is understood to be will be examined in more detail in the next section.

Finally, it is worthwhile pointing out the increasing role played by English in IPS and AFP. English was not the predominant language in either of these news agencies, but has increasingly been gaining importance in both organizations, not only in relation to news production and output but also with respect to organizational matters and news models. In the case of AFP, this has gone hand in hand with its expansion in the North American and Asian markets from the 1980s, and is expressed in the appointment of an Anglophone editor-in-chief in 1999. Significantly, the growing importance of English in the organization is not merely related to the production of more texts in that language, but also to attempts at the harmonization of criteria among the different newswires which favour the Anglophone model based on the use of shorter, more concise and direct texts to the detriment of the French or Spanish models, in which rhetoric and a literary style are more important.

In IPS, English has become key in reaching a new kind of reader directly through the internet, although Spanish media still predominate among subscribers. Spanish has in theory the same importance as English, but in practice references to the global service implicitly designate the latter, while the Spanish service is considered a regional, Latin American service.[1] English is also gradually replacing Spanish as the organization's internal working language: while it used to be necessary to learn Spanish, now global meetings take place in English. IPS' prize for its best published feature, in which now only articles written or translated into English can participate, reflects this gradual change towards the assumption of English as the organization's first language.

Translating agency news: values and strategies

Having presented the nature and characteristics of regional desks and established the character of the dominant and the minority model of translation in news agencies, this section will approach translation practices in more detail, discussing specific values and strategies and analysing the views of the journalists themselves. A comparative element will be retained in order to explain different perspectives in the two organizations, but news translation will also be discussed more generally in relation to the nature of the journalistic text produced at news agencies.

First of all, as we have already seen, news translation can entail the thoroughgoing transformation of the source text and the production of a new one designed to suit specific audiences according to the journalistic norms of the region. Journalists need to view the source text not as a finished product, but as the basis for the elaboration of a new text which will convey the information required to new readers with maximum efficiency. A very good illustration of how the source text is treated in news translation is the following:

The head of one foreign desk in Europe tells his staff to approach the translation process as if the base English-language copy were a press statement. Any journalist worth his or her salt would never simply reproduce a press statement. The basic facts are there. But the order often has to be rearranged. This is especially true of press statements where the real (especially if it's bad) news is often tucked away at the bottom. Relevant background needs to be added to a press statement and the same might be the case when rendering an English story more relevant or comprehensible to the local target audience.

(Williams, 2004)

The fact that agency news is unsigned also helps to promote this view of the source text as raw material rather than as a finished piece of news, and to allow for the possibility of altering structure and contents in important ways. Even in the case of IPS, where news features are signed, there is space for considerable modification, as authorship, which is considered sacred in the literary field, does not have the same status in the journalistic medium.

The available space for modification is nowhere more evident than in the work of news translators who adapt source texts for a very different, geographically distant readership. In AFP, this is especially the case of the two French editors, who produce French-language syntheses of events in Latin America for the French public. Their title is 'regional journalist for Latin America' and their task is a hybrid one, as they translate news reports into French – mainly from offices where no French journalists are present, but also texts of a wider regional scope which could not be put together by international correspondents working in one particular country – and are also regularly sent to cover events as reporters. They must follow the development of events in the whole Latin American region and, at the desk, their task is to select from the Spanish newswire items that might be of interest for the French public and to translate them. Their work is marked by the prevailing context of a relatively low interest of the French media in the region, which can be illustrated with the fact that few French newspapers still maintain their own correspondents in Latin America. In turn, this makes their job all the more important, as AFP has become one of the most significant sources of information about the region for the French-speaking public.

The translations of the French editors at Montevideo's regional desk, which are edited in Paris's international desk, incorporate significant changes, as it is often necessary to add relevant background for the European public. In addition, texts have to be adapted to the style and the journalistic norms of a different context. Often more than one source text is used for the elaboration of a news report which is not only a translation but also a synthesis of different news texts related to one particular theme (this is also a frequent practice with English-language translators at IPS). One of the French editors used the metaphor of film, with a script that cannot be changed but requiring that the translator acts like a director in establishing a focus and mixing the scenes in a particular way, to illustrate his task. In this case, the obligation towards the source text is one of preserving the 'spirit of the text' in the widest sense: retaining the aims of the reporter who wrote it while transforming the text in such a way that a French reader can understand it and relate to the reality it describes.

In fact, their task is not substantially different than that of the Spanish-language editors who translate from the French and English newswires for the Spanish-speaking public and similarly rewrite their texts so as to make them suitable for different contexts and new readers who are geographically distant from where the narrated events took place. However – like the journalists dealing with the subjects of economy and society – the French editors work more autonomously than their colleagues of the Spanish-language service and themselves select the texts to be translated. The choice of texts is based upon knowledge of client needs (through reading the European press and also personally monitoring which of their notes are taken up and where) and upon journalistic criteria of news relevance and the high media interest in certain subjects and themes, such as science and society, archaeology, history, environment, indigenous peoples or also the involvement of European actors in the narrated events.

At the Spanish desk, dispatches to be edited and translated are selected and distributed to the editors by one of the journalists who acts as desk chief. Spanish-language editing and translation from French and English into Spanish are thus not treated as different processes but rather assumed by journalists indistinctively. The task of the desk chief, who follows more closely the main themes of the day and tends to be less directly engaged in translation, is primarily one of coordination and distribution of the flow of information. Dispatches dealing with related themes are often assigned to the same person, who knows the information better and can detect any errors more easily when revising translations.

The established editorial priorities and previsions of the day discussed at the editorial meeting are the first reference for the selection of texts to be translated, in combination with the constant generation of urgent information. Other main criteria are related to geographical location (proximity to Latin America), and to the relevance of information for the region and knowledge of client needs: dispatches must not be too local with reference to European or North American events, and certain themes, such as institutional information from Washington,[2] always tend to be translated.

At IPS, news editors and translators-editors themselves select the texts they translate. In this organization, considerations related to an editorial policy based on inclusion are important with respect to both themes and regions. Thus, an explicit policy at Montevideo's Spanish desk is to translate more information about Africa, after perceiving that the region has an insufficient presence in the Spanish news service. The weekly editorial meeting also serves to establish thematic priorities and to detect inadequate coverage. More generally, dispatches must be of a regional, rather than local, character and, according to a translator-editor of the English service, of interest to an English-speaking global audience. Other criteria for selection are explicitly related to the quality of the dispatch itself, which must have its own sources and develop an appropriate analysis, and to the temporal factor (events described must be recent) and timeliness of the dispatch.

Journalists working at the desk have a very different perspective on the process of news production than reporters in the field. As one editor remarks, their job is basically ensuring that the information they receive is accurate and that it describes effectively the development of events; that sources are correct and the order in which events are narrated follows an inverted pyramid structure. This applies generally to edition work. According to an IPS editor, 'The task of translating a dispatch is not very different from the task of editing a dispatch in Spanish. The only difference is that the original is in a different language.' By this, we must understand not only that translation also implies the task of editing, but also that both are equally subject to the journalistic norms governing the production of news. Translation and editing ensure that information is presented in a correct, concise and comprehensible way, and that it is devoid of unnecessary elements and describes the facts to readers in the most direct manner possible.

However, translation implies not only editing of texts, but a further task of transformation to ensure that information is especially designed to suit the needs of new audiences. This involves a significant amount of reorganizing and rewriting of information according to a new hierarchy that reflects the needs and priorities of the target clients and the region to which it is destined. An IPS translator-editor described her role in this process as follows:

> We decide which notes to translate into English and we translate them for the English-speaking market, thinking of this market, of this audience. We add context, re-edit, reorganize the note, we give it a new title. We do a lot of work with the note; it rarely is a direct translation, just as it comes … We even combine notes if there are two or three about a subject when we do not need three notes in English on that subject.

As mentioned above, the French editors at AFP also described this as current practice, and AFP's Spanish editors similarly refer to necessary alterations like the addition of background knowledge to suit the Latin American client and changing the priority of elements in the dispatch, such as highlighting references to any country in the Latin American region and moving them to the top, even when they might originally have appeared at the end of the note. Their main task is thus one of selection, discrimination and prioritization, a work of synthesis which allows them to render the more relevant elements of the English and French services to their Spanish-language clients in a more compact form.

If conciseness and clarity are the main objectives of this two-fold task of edition/translation through which texts are not only checked and corrected but also synthesized and rewritten for a new public, the main strategy to achieve them is fluency. An IPS English-language translator-editor states that her aim is that notes can be read as if they were originally written in English and not as translations, while a colleague of the Spanish-language service states the same with respect to Spanish-language notes. Generally, journalists emphasize that translations must be easy to read and to understand, they must not use unnecessary words and vocabulary has to be kept simple. Journalists at both organizations also stress that context is of primary importance: the note must contain all necessary information so that readers do not need to fall back on other sources in order to understand it fully. For example, an AFP editor stated: 'What I want is that translated information can be read on its own, that the reader does not need to have recourse to a newspaper, a dictionary or the internet in order to understand it.' Another editor at AFP mentioned that information has to be translated in such a way that it can be published without adding or changing anything, while also emphasizing precision, which in agency journalism becomes paramount especially in the case of quotes. More generally, faithfulness to the original text and to the personal vision of its author is also emphasized, in spite of the wide scope for alteration and rewriting. Respecting the reporters' own analysis of facts is seen as especially relevant in the case of signed notes, which are common in IPS and a product for which there is a growing demand among the Latin American clients of AFP.

Editing translated texts is a common practice among journalists, especially in AFP, where all translations must always be seen by a second pair of eyes. The way journalists evaluate and edit translations also indicates the most relevant translating strategies and values at news agencies. Initially, the quality of a translation can be assessed without having recourse to the original on two different levels: on the one hand, with regard to the appropriate use of a journalistic style (conciseness and correctness of headline and lead, inverted pyramid structure) and with reference to a coherent, clear, concise and logical narration of events; on the other hand, at the level of language and syntax, translations must not be too literal, must use a natural language that can be understood in the whole region and are also checked for false friends and incorrect expressions. A second revision compares the translated text to the original in order to verify numbers, dates, quantities and similar data, as well as to check that quotes have been translated faithfully and accurately. In addition, the desk chief also checks texts with reference to similar ones that have already been transmitted by the agency with the view to homogenize expressions and concepts and present a coherent product to the client.

As we know, agency dispatches are destined for other journalists rather than the general public: to radio, television and newspaper editors who might decide to pick up some information and transmit it to their audience after having adapted and modified it to suit their particular needs and style.

The neutrality, objectivity and impartiality of agency dispatches, which appear as raw, colourless information, as well as their inverted pyramid structure, are designed to suit a wide range of client preferences and to allow for adaptation of the product to different media uses.

With respect to objectivity and impartiality, various AFP editors identify the influence of Anglophone journalism, which in their opinion turns news agencies into mere transmitters of information which already exists, where journalists do not have a voice, and generates dependence on textual quotes from informants in order to convey interpretations of events. This contrasts with practices in the region, as Latin America has a long tradition of journalism linked to political interests. On the other hand, many editors point at objectivity as a questionable concept, which is made impossible by the mere selection of themes, the necessity to adopt a point of view and the prioritization of certain sources. Objectivity, in their view, must be rather understood in the sense of impartiality, which is a key attribute of agency output. Impartiality is defined primarily as a question of balance so that the text effectively reflects a complex and disputed reality. The issue of sources is also central in achieving a balanced portrayal of events. With respect to translation, objectivity is seen as transmitting the ideas of the original text accurately and faithfully.

On the other hand, subscribing news organizations are necessary mediators between the news agencies and the public. News agencies offer their media clients products which are ready to be broadcast or published without any alterations or additions, so agency journalists must work as if the information was reaching the final reader directly: agency dispatches must be fully edited, complete and correct and clearly understandable without any necessary additions. Nevertheless, the fact that agency dispatches are not destined for the general public but for other journalists in the first instance is, in the view of many editors, also important in determining how agency notes are written. Agency journalists must offer news editors a Latin American vision which is their own and treat information as a work in progress – never as a finished product – through the development of information as it unfolds in such a way that the editor always knows what to expect. To work for news editors rather than for general readers means, according to various editors, that demands are higher in terms of rigour and precision, which is an expression of news agencies' special responsibilities as news sources, and can also determine how key elements, such as title and lead, are formulated to attract the attention of the editor.

News agencies' special significance as news sources has been indicated in the previous chapter. In many cases, this means that they are the first to approach and describe new realities and have to find adequate concepts to deal with them, determining the expressions that will be widely used by other media. That is why there is a constant effort to homogenize criteria within and across the different newswires and to achieve consistency and offer a coherent approach. However, agencies are often obliged to negotiate or change the terms used to offer an initial interpretation of events. A news editor gave an example in which a literal Spanish translation of the US operation in Afghanistan 'infinite justice' ('justicia infinita'), was circulated for several hours until it was changed to the terms 'justicia perdurable' ('long-lasting justice'), giving it a slightly different emphasis. At the same time, however, news agencies are also bound by the terms and formulas that predominate in other media, and might need to rectify their uses accordingly. Agency manuals contain long lists of proper names and other potentially rare or problematical terms designed to facilitate this task.

News agencies' task of describing events worldwide as they take place is subject to two key attributes: accuracy and speed. Speed has always been an important part of agency journalism, which is all about offering factual information on events in the shortest possible time and has traditionally revolved about getting there first, beating the competition and obtaining precious information on breaking news and scoops. Each news agency has its own story of glorious scoops, when the inventiveness and resilience of reporters were rewarded with the achievement of exclusive information ahead of all competitors. Reuters had a seventy-minute break in announcing the shooting of Gandhi in 1948, while one of AFP's most famous scoops was the announcement of the death of the Israeli hostages during the 1972 Munich Olympics, fifty-six minutes ahead of others. A reporter who stayed behind obtained the information from the city mayor, who refuted an earlier official version that they had been saved. The fact that some dailies that did not subscribe to AFP appeared the morning after with news of the liberation of the hostages on their front page illustrates how important this kind of struggle with time and speed to provide accurate information on breaking news can be.

Decades ago, when the transmission of information depended on less advanced technology, trying to get to the phone or the telegraph first, and making access for others more difficult, were common practices among correspondents. One UPI journalist got to the phone he shared with his colleague from AP first when Kennedy was shot in Dallas, and purposely delayed the latter's transmission by holding on to it. Until recently, common practices among journalists also included bribing officials in telegraph offices or pretending that working phones were out of order.

Today, technology allows for the ever faster transmission of information reaching near-instantaneous coverage of events as they take place, which is expressed in the continuous coverage and updating of breaking news by channels of continuous information and internet sites. This general acceleration of the pace of the circulation of information places new demands on news sources and an increasing pressure is felt at the news agencies to fulfil client expectations for real-time information. Newspapers' closing time has ceased to be a reference for news agency output, which must satisfy the varied information needs of different types of clients at any time of the day.

The pressures derived from time and speed directly affect translation practices in news agencies. An AFP desk chief described the situation as follows:

> People at the agency work at a very accelerated pace ... A journalist here processes between twenty and forty texts daily to which I must pay attention, of which four or five are translations. Speed leads you to produce errors, to a more literal translation, to changing meanings and contexts. It is very limiting. And it is also true that everything is accelerating even more. Some years ago a newspaper could wait for an analysis ... Today, a newspaper in Quito wants to receive immediately an analysis of the oil problem that an English newspaper is publishing today or is going to publish tomorrow ... There are complex translations, but it is difficult to have more than an hour to do them. To translate 600 words in an hour and guarantee that the translation is good is very complicated.

It is also necessary to keep in mind that pressures vary depending on the urgency of information: there is generally less time (and consequently less space for modification and rewriting) for urgent information, which must be circulated within a few minutes and which tends to be translated word for word.

Nevertheless, it would be wrong to assume that the need to work at great speed ultimately undermines the production of accurate news. On the contrary, speed is seen as an intrinsic part of the process of news translation, as an element of journalistic quality. A news editor at AFP stated that 'to translate means to translate fast, well and accurately', while another one pointed out that 'speed is part of the job'. Arguably, journalistic translation must incorporate a rhythm that distinguishes it from other forms of translation, in which full syntactic and grammatical correction might be deemed more important. A senior member of the IPS team identified speed and adrenaline as specific to news agency journalism and emphasized that 'Speed is as important as quality, it is part of quality. Maybe [the text] comes out with mistakes, it might not be perfect, but it has to come out fast.' Guaranteeing both speed and accuracy, in spite of the inherent contradictions that this might originate, is part of the task of news agencies which, as has been pointed out in the previous chapter, must always correct inadequate or mistaken information (including mistranslations) in order to maintain their credibility as sources of information.

As we have seen, the pace of work is not as accelerated at IPS, where a translation usually takes two hours to complete, which is slow for the market average, and editors have a quota of five texts (including both editions and translations) a day. A translator-editor explains IPS' approach and its consequences for translation as follows:

> IPS has increasingly moved into the timeless note, which is our niche: a note with context, with an angle, with a different focus from mainstream

media. With these notes we are not so pressured. But we do need to have something in the English wire on Latin America as soon as possible and in a sustained way during the day, and then there are the more urgent notes ... As we are not going to be first or second, generally we try offer something good, with a different focus, the necessary context and sources, sources from civil society, from the people who do not have a voice.

However, the pressures that dictate the timely appearance of texts, and which differentiate journalistic translation from other types of translation, also apply. Thus, in the view of IPS' regional editor for Latin America, the features and analysis produced:

> are more lengthy notes with a lot of context, with data that must be corroborated, etc., and the translation takes much longer. But we have production quotas, timetables, and especially in recent times we are fighting to modify certain work habits ... There is a great difference between the fast translation of a dispatch of four or five paragraphs and literary translation or the translation of an essay or of scientific works. IPS is not dedicated to literature or to scientific work; we produce news that has to be published in newspapers and on the internet and that is going to be read today or tomorrow and no more. Then, beyond all the values that an article might have, our work needs to have essentially a journalistic rhythm.

The journalist: an invisible translator?

Reflecting once more on the issue of the translator's invisibility in the specific context of news production can offer an approximation to the role played by translation in the journalistic field as well as an indication of what distinguishes news translation from other forms of translation. This time, however the starting point for this reflection are the opinions on this matter of the journalists themselves, who gave answers in their interviews to an open-ended question posed by the researcher on the invisibility of translation in the field of news.

On the one hand, some editors remarked that translation has to be invisible, not only because translations are unsigned, but also because invisibility guarantees the good quality of the translation which, like edition, has to respect the work and vision of the original producer of the news. An editor stated, in this respect:

> In news agencies I have never seen that translators figure explicitly. Editors don't figure either. We have an internal system of codification in which responsibility is indicated with the initials in each process; that is, the author, the editor, the translator. But this is for internal consumption and the public doesn't see it, so it remains totally invisible. Much more

so than the editor, because ultimately the editor is the one who has to face things or who receives letters from the readers. On the contrary, the translator as such doesn't.

In this context, a translator-editor also remarked that translators 'are more invisible than editors, because you can understand what the editor is doing ... People don't generally understand that there are also translators. Notes are read as if they were written by a native English speaker. We are thus invisible.'

On the other hand, translation's invisibility is questioned by editors who point to the specific forms of textual intervention on the part of news translators:

> In news, I don't know to which extent [translation] is so invisible, because we are directly transforming a reality that comes from a different context for a public whose characteristics we believe we know. I think that in many cases the journalistic sense of the translator prevails. As translator, there isn't the freedom to re-elaborate everything in a text, but certain nuances can be added, even important ones.
>
> ... invisible as a strict reflection of events, but in reality it is fifty-fifty, because information needs to be oriented to make it attractive to a regional public. So, not intervening in the news in the sense that you add or eliminate data, but intervening in the orientation, in hierarchization. It is about intervening, maybe not in the translation itself, but in what is called prioritization.

This type of intervention is related to three main tasks that are assumed as part of the process of translation. First, a task of selection and synthesis, through which only that information which is considered to be relevant is rendered in the target language. Second, a task of prioritization of information, through which the original text is adapted to the needs of the new audience. Third, a task of changing news angles and nuances, when the new informative context justifies it. We saw in the previous chapter that the possibility of changing news angles in order to better fulfil the needs and expectations of a different audience pushes the very notion of equivalence to its limit, revealing how different versions of global news events can function in very diverse local contexts. The translator's visibility and transformative role in news production is directly related to this power to actually change the prevalent news angle or point of view from which events are narrated in order to produce a new text which can function more effectively as news for a different public.

With respect to news agency production, there emerges in this context an important paradox between the need to harmonize criteria in the different newswires so that they respond to a consistent editorial politics of the organization as a whole, and the need to adapt to cultural, geographic and linguistic difference. A news agency needs to present a coherent vision of the world in spite of linguistic and regional differences, and daily coordination between the regions is destined to ensure the prevalence of this unity of focus, which is permanently threatened by the constant generation of urgent information. However, on the other hand, the emphasis and news angle that prevail in each region are determined by local circumstances, and need to be tailored to each specific context in order to make texts successfully function as news. This paradox is at the very core of this kind of global organization which also maintains a local presence in many countries and ultimately very difficult to resolve.

A good example of arising conflicts with respect to news angle arose with the coverage of Ronald Reagan's funeral during fieldwork at AFP's Montevideo regional centre. English-language notes from Washington were translated at this office and the divergence was clearly visible when articles celebrating and praising the life and achievements of a respected head of state had to be rendered in Spanish, in a region where this figure, associated with one of the most aggressive periods of US foreign policy and the dirty wars in Central America, has sinister connotations. In this context, adding background information related to Reagan's economic policies and to his participation in the wars in Nicaragua, El Salvador and Guatemala was much more significant to the Latin American media reader than narrating the ex-president's last look of love to his wife.

In spite of constant coordination and, maybe even more significantly, of the growing influence of Anglophone journalism in news agencies, continuing differences of style and content, of focus and priority prevail in their different newswires. The task of news translation is one of successfully dealing with these differences while, at the same time, making it possible that information can successfully circulate across linguistic, cultural and geographical boundaries.

6 Reading translated news
An analysis of agency texts

Chapters 4 and 5 have provided a general framework for the analysis of news translation and a description of current practices in news agencies. This chapter centres on agency texts and uses textual analysis in order to reflect on the nature of translation in news agencies.

News agencies' task of describing events worldwide as they take place implies, as we have seen, the constant generation of textual output, which is permanently revised and updated according to new developments. This principle of constant textual production is clearly expressed in AFP's *Manual of the Spanish Service*:

> Resulta obvio decir que siempre hay en algún lugar del mundo un lector consultando Internet o el WAP de su teléfono celular, un cliente que está cerrando sus páginas o consultando su pantalla para tomar decisíones antes de comenzar su noticiero de radio o televisión.
>
> Esta realidad impone no solamente actuar deprisa, sino también trabajar de modo que no haya 'agujeros negros', es decir, que pasen varias horas sin que la agencia informe sobre los temas del día o los que van a serlo. Para ello, es necesario organizar programas de cobertura que incluyan notas previas, notas sucesivas, análisis y papeles de seguimiento. No se trata de repetir más o menos mecánicamente el mismo papel, sino de encontrar ángulos o géneros capaces de mantener el interés de nuestros clientes.
>
> (2000: 37)

(It seems obvious to say that there are always readers somewhere in the world looking at the internet or at the WAP of their mobile phones, clients closing their pages or consulting their screens in order to take decisions before starting a news broadcast on radio or television.

This reality makes it imperative not only that we need to work fast, but also that we have to do so without leaving any 'black holes', that is, not to let several hours go by without the agency informing about the themes of the day or those which are going to become the themes of the day. In order to do this, it is necessary to programme coverage so as to include previous leads, subsequent leads, analyses and follow-ups. It is not a matter of repeating more or less automatically the same paper, but of finding angles and genres which are capable of maintaining the interest of our clients.)

From this quote we can also discern the central importance of new technologies, and especially the internet, in determining news agency output, and in particular in modifying the timetable and pace of information production, which was previously adapted to the peaks of newspapers' closing times but which now seeks to accommodate to a global internet user 24/7. Although there is a sprawl of bibliography examining the impact of new media on journalism (see, for example, Gunter 2003; Harper 1998; Kawamoto 2003; Pavlik 2001), a systematic study of the influence of the internet on news agencies is still lacking.

The distinction between wholesale information producers (the news agencies) and information retailers has been relativized and redrawn in the past decades. Not only have new types of media organizations appeared that assume the tasks of production for sale to other media and of direct communication with the public at the same time (the channels of continuous information), but traditional wholesalers have also started to approach the public directly. In this latter development the internet is of primary importance and has generated very different responses from the various news agencies. Reuters has embraced the internet to offer a wide selection of its news to the general public, without any viewing restrictions. AFP's approach is very different: the organization offers a strictly limited selection of news in its different formats (news reports, pictures and teletype news), with the objective to publicize the type of product available rather than to provide information to the wider public. IPS has fully embraced the internet and is no longer distributed through teletype. Its news products are available to the general public through its webpage, although passwords are required for a limited number of articles and to access the online archives.

In addition, news agencies offer online products with multimedia news for websites, including online reports and online newspapers in several languages, as well as news selections which are emailed to clients according to their specific needs. Online news services are finished products ready to be incorporated by clients into their websites through a simple cut and paste operation. As we saw in Chapter 3, news agencies not only offered raw information which could be reworked by specific media clients according to their own needs, but also increasingly produced a variety of media products ready to publish or air without the need of any modification. Online news services are an extreme form of this tendency, and websites, much in a similar way as small newspapers which incorporate agency reports without altering them in any way, are at the other pole of the big newspapers that basically use news agencies as raw information providers.

The internet not only facilitates customization through a number of news services 'à la carte', but also the circulation and general availability of news in a growing number of languages, and news agencies increasingly spend time translating for their internet services. At AFP's regional office in Montevideo, two journalists are ordinarily dedicated to translating news for AFP's online newspaper *¡AFP Ya!*. Reuters' Madrid office houses, in addition to a Spanish desk, an online desk, where Spain's online service is produced. According to a journalist of the Spanish service, the production of the online desk is predominantly based on translation, with about 80 per cent of its output, while only 20 per cent is original Spanish-language production. This relationship is reversed in the case of the Spanish desk. This journalist also describes how the internet has generated new information needs, and in particular a larger demand for local information:

> There was an explosion of information destined for the internet. Online desks that previously didn't exist were created. Spain's online desk started with two people, who basically translated material to send to websites, and now there are six or seven people in a service from seven in the morning to eleven at night, including weekends. In some countries we have twenty-four hour service.

The internet has made possible news agencies' new role as direct information providers to the public and its influence is revealed in the samples of agency texts analysed in this chapter, the main objectives of which are to explore the patterns of linguistic diversity in the dissemination of agency texts and to analyse in detail how specific texts are translated. The sheer volume of agency output makes an investigation of this kind extremely difficult and this analysis has consequently been based on three small samples of texts from different organizations, each illuminating different aspects related to language and translation in news agencies. The first section deals with a variety of texts collected at AFP's regional office in Montevideo during fieldwork in June 2004. This unsystematic sample is used to illustrate the main features of different kinds of agency texts and the role played by translation in their production. The second sample gathers news texts published on Reuters' websites in English, Spanish and French, describing how news texts circulate within one particular organization as well as the basic operations of news translation as they can be discerned from an examination of news material made available to the public on a specific date. The third sample offers a systematic study of IPS' coverage of the 2004 World Social Forum in English, Spanish and Dutch, and identifies the effects of an alternative politics of language and translation on news production.

The translation of agency news: a sample of AFP texts

The nature and structure of agency news can best be described by following the development of an item of urgent information. The death of singer Ray Charles was announced on 10 June 2004 by a concise bulletin which cited his publicist as source. This was immediately followed by an urgent and, minutes later, by the first lead.[1] These were all speedily translated into other languages, and the time between the appearance of the English-language text and its Spanish and French translations was never more than five minutes.

The urgent, circulated at 16.38 GMT, specified for the first time the cause of death as well as significant background details, including Ray Charles' age, and set the structure for all subsequent information as follows:

> Legendary singer Ray Charles dead at 73: publicist
>   LOS ANGELES, Jun 10 (AFP) – Legendary musician Ray Charles, dubbed the 'Genius of Soul,' died Thursday as a result of complications from liver disease, his publicist told AFP. He was 73.

Only three minutes later the Spanish and French translations appeared:

> El legendario cantante Ray Charles muere a los 73 años
>   LOS ANGELES, Jun 10 (AFP) – El legendario músico Ray Charles, conocido como 'el genio del soul', falleció este jueves a los 73 años como resultado de una enfermedad que le afectaba el hígado, dijo su agente de prensa a la AFP.

> Le chanteur de jazz Ray Charles est mort
>   LOS ANGELES, 10 juin (AFP) – Le chanteur et musicien de jazz américain Ray Charles, surnommé 'le génie de la soul', est mort jeudi à l'âge de 73 ans de complications d'une maladie du foie, a annoncé son agent à l'AFP.

The inverted pyramid structure of agency news, in which the most important information comes in the first paragraphs and in descending order, means that this information was retained in subsequent, longer texts, which added background and details. Thus, the English-language lead circulated at 16.41 was:

> Legendary singer Ray Charles dead at 73: publicist
>   LOS ANGELES, Jun 10 (AFP) – Legendary musician Ray Charles, dubbed the 'Genius of Soul,' died Thursday as a result of complications from liver disease, his publicist told AFP. He was 73.
>   The Grammy-award winning crooner died at 11:35 am (1835 GMT) in his Beverly Hills home, Jerry Digney said. He was surrounded by family and friends.

The second paragraph of the text adds the time and place of death. The singer's trajectory, already introduced in his characterization as a Grammy award winner, was the object of further extensions of this first lead and of the second lead, which appeared as a signed text of 449 words half an hour later, adding quotes, details and background. This text already offered a full piece of news in agency flavour, specifying the most relevant facts of Charles' death and illness as well as providing an outline of his trajectory. It was translated into Spanish and French in very similar terms. At the same time, a whole series of related texts, such as biographical summaries and profiles, were also circulated and translated into the different newswires.

Agency translations tend to be fast and reliable renderings of factual information, with minimal amounts of modification. However, it is easy to introduce, even in the context of literal translations, significant differences and to reinforce certain nuances. For example, on 10 June 2004 a lead announcing the death of two young Palestinians at the hands of Israeli troops was circulated in French, English and Spanish. The French and Spanish versions specify in their title that the two victims were teenagers ('Deux adolescents palestiniens tués par des soldats israéliens en Cisjordanie' and 'Dos adolescentes palestinos muertos por soldados Israelíes en Cisjordania'), while the English title omits this information ('Two Palestinians killed by Israeli troops in West Bank'), which only appears in its opening paragraph. The only other modification to an otherwise literal translation of a short piece of information (less than 200 words) is the specification, in the French and Spanish versions, that the first victim was shot during a raid by seven military jeeps in the Ras al Aïn area of Nablus, while the English version only mentions that 'troops raided the northern town of Nablus'.

Information concerning violence against the Palestinians has similar news relevance in the English, French and Spanish wires, justifying therefore few alterations of length and detail and in many cases giving origin to close or literal translations of news reports. The case is different with translations that convey information for more distant publics than those targeted by the original piece of news, for example, of French versions of Spanish-language news about Latin America, which require a higher degree of modification of a source text that must necessarily be adapted to the needs of the French media market and readers. In order to appreciate the sort of changes involved, a short text of these characteristics is reproduced in full in its original Spanish and its French version:

Cervecería guatemalteca producirá cerveza para seguidores de ciencia ficción

GUATEMALA, Jun 11 (AFP) – La Cervecería Centroamericana (CCA), de capital guatemalteco, fue contratada por los estudios estadounidenses Paramount Pictures para producir una cerveza dedicada a los seguidores de películas o series de ciencia ficción, informó este viernes un representante de la firma.

La cerveza, cuyo nombre será Romulan Ale, será de color azul debido a que corresponde al color oficial de los filmes integalácticos, indicó el jefe de exportaciones de la compañía guatemalteca, Jimmie Shepherd.

'Fue un verdadero reto hacer la cerveza con ese color sin que perdiera su sabor original', aseguró.

'Por lo menos cuatro veces al año, los fieles seguidores de Star Wars y Star Trek se reúnen en Estados Unidos en grandes convenciones', donde será vendido el nuevo producto, agregó, pero no reveló la cantidad que se producirá anualmente.

De acuerdo con Shepherd, Cervecería Centroamericana fue seleccionada debido a los premios a nivel mundial que ha ganado la elaboración de su producto líder 'Cerveza Gallo'.

El empresario comentó que la firma también fue contratada por la cadena alemana Aldi para que produzca y distribuya las cervezas Monterrey y Light en más de 700 sucursales en Estados Unidos.

(Guatemalan beer manufacturer will produce beer for science fiction fans

GUATEMALA, Jun 11 (AFP) – Cervecería Centroamericana (CCA), of Guatemalan capital, was hired by the North American Paramount Pictures to produce a beer dedicated to science fiction film or series fans, a representative of the firm informed this Friday.

The beer, named Romulan Ale, will be blue as this is the official colour of intergalactic films, the chief of exports of the Guatemalan company, Jimmie Shepherd, indicated.

'It was a true challenge to make the beer in this colour without it losing its original taste', he asserted.

'At least four times a year, the faithful fans of Star Wars and Star Trek gather in the United States in large conventions', where the new product will be sold, he added, without revealing the amount that will be produced annually.

According to Shepherd, Cervecería Centroamericana was selected due to the prizes at the international level the manufacturing of its leading product 'Cerveza Gallo' has won.

The businessman mentioned that the firm has also been hired by the German chain Aldi to produce and distribute the Monterrey and Light beers in more than 700 branches in the United States.)

Une bière bleue pour les amateurs des films et séries de science fiction

GUATEMALA, 11 juin (AFP) – Une brasserie guatémaltèque va produire de la bière de couleur bleue à la demande de Paramount Pictures (cinéma), filiale du groupe américain Viacom Entertainment Group, pour les amateurs de films et de séries de science-fiction, a annoncé vendredi un représentant du fabricant de boisson.

Selon le chef du département exportation de l'entreprise guatémaltèque, Jimmie Shepherd, la couleur bleue est la couleur officielle des fans de Star Wars et de Star Trek, célèbres film et série de télévision, qui se réunissent 'Du moins quatre fois paran lors de grands rassemblements aux Etats-Unis', où la bière sera vendue.

'Cela a été un véritable défi de faire de la bière de cette couleur sans perdre son goût original', a-t-il dit, sans révéler la quantité qui sera produite annuellement.

(A blue beer for science fiction film and series fans
   GUATEMALA, 11 June (AFP) – A Guatemalan brewery will produce blue beer at the demand of Paramount Pictures (film), a subsidiary of the American Viacom Entertainment Group, for science fiction films and series lovers, announced on Friday a representative of the drink manufacturer.
   According to the chief of the exports division of the Guatemalan firm, Jimmie Shepherd, blue is the official colour of fans of Star Wars and Star Trek, famous film and television series, who get together 'at least four times a year' in large conventions in the United States, where the beer will be sold.
   'To make a beer in this colour without losing its original taste has been a real challenge,' he said, without revealing the amount that will be produced annually.)

In the French version, the usual modifications of a translation that relies on a domesticating strategy which privileges fluency and transparency and conformance to the expectations of the target reader can be observed: change of title (for the French media, the most important fact is the production of blue beer and not that a company from Guatemala produces it), omission of less relevant information (the names of the beer and of its manufacturing company are not rendered in French; the two final paragraphs are left out), addition of information (the French version specifies that Paramount Pictures is a subsidiary of Viacom Entertainment Group). Agency style, and in particular the inverted pyramid structure which presents information according to a strict hierarchy, facilitates translation and in this case the less relevant information appearing at the end of the Spanish text is omitted in the shorter French version. Also conforming to agency style, quotes from informants are maintained and privileged as sources. But the French version modifies the text according to its news relevance and to the background knowledge of readers in a new context; it is also significantly an exercise of subtle rewriting through which the original text is rendered in the most efficient form. To this end, paragraphs are recombined (paragraph one of the French version contains information given in the first two paragraphs of the Spanish text) and reorganized (the order of the two quotes is inverted and the informant's first statement is presented as the text's closure) in the production of a new version which substantially enhances the form and consistency of the original Spanish text.

As we saw in Chapter 5, translations of news texts for a public which is geographically removed from the reality where events have taken place, such as those produced by French regional editors for Latin America based in

Montevideo, often entail not just a considerable amount of rewriting of the original version, but also the combination of different source texts. One example of this kind is the article entitled 'Soumis à un referendum, Chávez lance sa contre-attaque' (Subjected to a referendum, Chávez launches his counter-attack), from 11 June 2004, which is a translation based on two different source texts: 'Las cartas de Hugo Chávez para afrontar el referendo revocatorio' (Hugo Chávez's cards to face a revoking referendum), from 10 June 2004 (source text A), and 'Chávez busca aliados en los libros de historia para ganar referendo' (Chávez seeks allies from history books to win referendum), from 11 June 2004 (source text B). Interestingly, both articles are signed by their author, Tibisay Soto, and the signature is maintained in the French version. The French translation reworks and completely reorganizes the two source texts, of 747 and 790 words respectively, into a new version of 651 words. It also significantly alters the contents, clarifying information where necessary, adding relevant context details and eliminating or modifying sentences. Its opening paragraph or lead is already a reinterpretation of the source text which introduces significant changes:

> Avec un discours guerrier et un budget gonflé par les pétrodollars, le président vénézuélien Hugo Chávez mobilise ses troupes plus de deux mois d'un référendum susceptible de le chasser du pouvoir, alors que sa cote de popularité est de 40%.

> (With a belligerent discourse and a budget swollen by petrodollars, the Venezuelan president Hugo Chávez mobilizes his troops more than two months before a referendum which could remove him from power, when his popularity rate is 40%.)

Source text A:

> Una popularidad del 40% tras cinco años de gobierno; control de un Estado con las arcas llenas; impactantes programas sociales; liderazgo indiscutido para sus seguidores e imagen carismática: Hugo Chávez tiene varias cartas para afrontar el referendo revocatorio del 15 de agosto.

> (A popularity of 40% after five years of government; control of a State with its coffers full; impressive social programmes; unquestioned leadership to his followers and charismatic image: Hugo Chávez has several cards to face the revoking referendum of 15 August.)

The original text's emphatic references to the strengths of Chávez's government are reformulated in more neutral terms, and mentions of its 'impressive' social programmes and of Chávez's charismatic image and leadership omitted. At the same time, the translation already introduces in its first sentence 'a belligerent discourse' ('avec un discours guerrier') the subject matter of source text B, which is further developed in the second paragraph on the creation of 'commando Maisanta' by President Chávez – a figure described for the new target readers as 'l'ex-militaire putschiste arriveé au pouvoir par les urnes en 1998' (the ex-military coup leader who was elected to power in 1998) – with the objective of achieving in the referendum twice the number of votes than the opposition. The text then goes with some detail into the historical references of Chávez's discourse, which are described in source text B. His rebel great-grandfather known as 'Maisanta', who fought the oligarchy at the end of the nineteenth century and the beginning of the twentieth, and Ezequiel Zamora (leader of the federal troops and winner of the famous battle of Santa Inés in 1859), are invoked and compared to Chávez's own political mission, in the context of numerous efforts from the opposition to remove him from power, including the 2002 coup. The French translation takes from source text B its account of the historical references of Chávez's discourse, but omits most direct quotations of the president, who is now referred to as 'the populist president', as well as an allusion by the Venezuelan president to the present 'anti-imperialist phase' of his Bolivarian revolution. It then returns to source text A, through an added sentence of transition which does not figure in any of the Spanish texts, to elaborate on statistical predictions of the results of the referendum and on the opinions of the directors of two data analysis companies.

Source text A devotes particular attention to Chávez's social programmes, which benefit the poorest sectors of the population, where Chávez draws his major support, and in which, following the commentators, Chávez is going to pour abundant resources. The French version quotes one of the analysts in this respect (but omits the description of these social programmes, which occupies several paragraphs in the source text), and also refers to Chávez's other 'hidden trumps': dividing the opposition and promoting abstention in order to retain his grip on power. It also adds a new paragraph specifying the number of votes that must be obtained for the opposition to win and returns in its closure to source text B with a reference to the opposition's debate on the designation of a single candidate.

In this example, translation entails a considerable amount of rewriting through which the source text is filtered and reconstituted in a new form, which effectively conveys the most important facts contained in both texts. In the process of translation, as we have already indicated in Chapter 4, a new angle can be emphasized or a particular emphasis changed, when the new context and target readers to which it is addressed justify it, and even close translations often introduce modifications of this kind. In the example above, Chávez's strengths were described in a more neutral way in the French version which, at the same time, characterized him as a populist president, a designation that would not be unfamiliar to European readers. At the same time, the role of the president's own discourse was minimized and the anti-imperialist references which ideologically justify his political programme completely omitted in order to privilege a more detached analysis of the situation based on observations from other relevant sources.

Another example of this kind of operation can be found in the texts dealing with Ronald Reagan's funeral. Our example is an article written originally in English entitled 'Reagan hailed for winning Cold War without firing a shot', which appeared on 11 June 2004, and its French and Spanish translations, entitled 'Reagan salué comme le vainqueur de la Guerre froide' and 'Funerales de Reagan convocaron a ex líderes de la Guerra Fría'. Strangely, the text appears as a signed feature (by Tim Witcher) in both its French and Spanish versions but not in its original English version. Written on the occasion of Reagan's state funeral, the article's main objective is to offer the testimonies of other principal actors of the Cold War period, who were all gathered at the ceremony. To this end, it contains a summary and various quotations from Lady Thatcher's speech at the funeral, as well as extracts from interviews with Gorbachev and Walesa which appeared in the *New York Times* and the *Wall Street Journal* respectively. This is accompanied by a brief overview of the relationship and gradual rapprochement between the two superpowers at the end of the Cold War.

The original text establishes early on the view of the ex-president as the winner of the Cold War, designating him in the first paragraph as 'the Great Liberator' and focusing in its central part on Lady Thatcher's presentation of Reagan as the leader of the free world against the 'evil empire' (as Reagan called the Soviet Union in 1983). The French and Spanish versions maintain the structure of the English text, but also nuance it significantly, as is already apparent in their respective titles. Most radically, the Spanish title changes the prevalent angle which commemorates Reagan as the winner of the Cold War and highlights instead the gathering of the main political leaders of the period. It also eliminates Reagan's designation as 'the Great Liberator' from the first paragraph, which only appears in paragraph 12 in a direct quotation from Lady Thatcher. Offering slightly shorter versions, the Spanish and French translations also omit some of the quotations from Lady Thatcher's speech and from Gorbachev at the end.

The purpose of news translation is to adapt texts to the needs of different publics, which requires not only reorganizing and contextualizing information, but also an exercise of subtle rewriting in order to heighten the effectiveness of the original text in the new context. Texts are marked by the local realities of which they are a part. The communicative purposes of news texts determine that a domesticating translation or the linguistic adaptation to the usage of the target language is the most appropriate translation strategy (Reiss, 2000). This implies not just a formal adaptation to the linguistic structures of the target language, but also a transformation of contents. For a European audience, Hugo Chávez is characterized as Venezuela's populist president, while his discourse is minimized in order to approach the reality of the country privileging other sources from the political spectrum in what is perceived to be a more balanced and neutral way of news reporting.

Similarly, to the Latin American public, which suffered the Cold War as America's backyard with great human loss, presenting Ronald Reagan's funeral as a gathering of Cold War leaders rather than celebrating the figure of the ex-president as its winner appears as a more meaningful form of commemoration.

The changing role of news agencies in the field of global news: Reuters' website

As has been indicated above, Reuters has used the internet to break with the traditional role of news agencies as wholesale producers of news for other media organizations. Reuters' internet strategy and the importance the organization attaches to becoming a direct source of information to the public are mirrored in the fact that its website is currently ranked amongst the world's first fifteen digital news media. If the channels of continuous information have eroded the traditional boundaries between wholesalers and retailers by selling their news to other media, the news agencies have responded by becoming, through the internet, retailers themselves, which leads Ignacio Muro Benayas to remark: 'Si las fronteras de la actividad entre las agencias y los medios estaban claras hace apenas una década, Internet los ha forzado a compartir, cada vez más, nuevos espacios y a competir por mercados fronterizos y competitivos' (2006: 148) (If the boundaries between the activity of the agencies and the media were clear only a decade ago, the internet has increasingly forced them to share new spaces and to compete for bordering and competitive markets).

As Muro Benayas points out, the internet promotes a new type of informative message that is especially close to the traditional values of instantaneity, conciseness and real-time information of the news agencies (2006: 147), which also helps to explain why these organizations (and Reuters in particular) have been able to use the technology so successfully. Indeed, if we return to the quotation from AFP's manual at the beginning of this chapter describing the need to produce constant and gradual information and to avoid any 'black holes', we can note a remarkable resemblance to the principles on which real-time internet news services 24/7 are based.

Most significantly, the blurring of the boundaries between the news agencies and other media is paralleled in the multimedia spaces inaugurated by the internet and the integration of text and audio-visual communication. The internet has become an important medium for the convergence of text, pictures and video in the presentation of news which increasingly combines several formats, including graphics and tables, and in which text is complemented by images and soundbites.

Reuters' website is a case in point. It combines general news with business news and a section on investment containing market and stocks news and indices. The weight of revenues obtained from economic services and general news services (the latter, as we have seen before, account for only 7 per cent of Reuters' income) is clearly not mirrored in the website, which gives special prominence to international news. Reuters' website offers text, pictures and links to video news, as well as graphs and share prices, and a very similar outlook is maintained in its eighteen localized editions, available in ten languages: English (UK, US, Canada, South Africa, India editions), Spanish (Spain, Latin America, Argentina and Mexico editions), Japanese, Chinese (traditional and simplified editions), Russian, French, German, Portuguese (Brazil edition), Arabic and Italian.

The US and UK websites contain the largest number of news. They are also markedly multimedia, offering special pages dedicated to video news and to news photography. For example, the latter contains the editor's choice of pictures of the last twenty-four hours as well as selections of 'picture stories' (series of photographs with captions describing particular events) and showcases of award-winning photographs and monthly selections. In other regional websites a small amount of photographs appears, always as a complement to text, and generally no video clips are made available (except in the Japanese website). Often, smaller editions such as those of Brazil, Argentina, Italy or South Africa contain no photographs at all.

Analysing news content on a particular date can reveal important features and offer a general picture of how news circulates globally through the organization's website. This sample is based on one day's news coverage (20 July 2006) in five websites (US, UK, Latin America, Spain and France) and three languages (English, Spanish and French). Ten news articles published in at least two different languages were found; constituting a total of twenty-six texts. The news of the day was marked by the ongoing war of Israel against Hizbollah in Lebanon, and most texts found in translation are related to this event, as well as to the evacuations of US and French citizens from the area and to other related issues (diplomatic relations between Israel and Spain; German spies' record of dealings with Hizbollah). Other news texts found in translation are about tsunami survivors in Java, the FIFA ban on football players Zidane and Materazzi, confrontations between Somali Islamists and Ethiopian troops, and the increasing numbers of refugees fleeing violence in Iraq.

The first thing to be noticed is a clear unidirectionality of translation from English into other languages. Most of the sampled texts are translations from English into Spanish and, in two cases, also from English into French. The only possible exception to this is a text dealing with the remarks of Israel's ambassador to Spain about the relationship between the two countries which was made available on Reuters British and Spanish websites, although it is not clear whether the text was originally written in Spanish or whether it was produced in English by an international journalist in Spain. Reuters' French website contains predominantly domestic news and incorporates remarkably fewer translations than either the Spanish or the Latin American websites. On the sampled date, Reuters' French website included two original French articles on the evacuation and repatriation of French citizens from Lebanon and a text on the bombing in Beirut. Significantly, these were not translated into other languages and were available only in the French website. Like the French website, Spain's website incorporates a considerable amount of domestic news, although international news has a stronger prominence. Latin America's website dedicates a page exclusively to international news in translation, while another one is destined for Latin American news.

In her analysis of English translations from *Der Spiegel*, available online in *Spiegel International*, Christina Schäffner argues that moving a text from print to a web-based environment requires translators to bear in mind the substantial differences between the two types of media, giving as examples the need to change photographs and their captions due to copyright regulations, and the elimination of footnotes, which can appear in the printed version (2005: 163–64). Similarly, in the case of agency texts, small alterations can be observed, such as the addition of subtitles in order to facilitate reception. However, the degree of modification is minimal, as texts for the website follow the same principles that regulate news agency output more generally: inverted pyramid structure and factual description of events with the inclusion of abundant quotes from relevant witnesses and informants. In addition, the website closely re-creates the pace that is characteristic of agency coverage of events as they take place by regularly publishing updates and indicating exactly the time elapsed since they have been made available, as well as by offering headlines of breaking news. However, only a certain kind of agency text tends to be selected for inclusion in the website: long articles, which are in most cases signed by a reporter. Short lead articles of around 400 words, which are very common on the newswire, do not tend to appear on the website. The website thus privileges an image of the news agency as producer of long informative articles by individual journalists – although traces of texts as a collective product can be seen at the end of reports, where the contribution of several other journalists is often credited.

Reuters' translations are made available through the website shortly after the original text appears and always on the same day. Generally, they retain the structure of the original, as well as the name of its author – although, it is needless to say, the name of the translator does not figure anywhere. The alterations discussed above as typical of news translation (elimination of information, reorganization of paragraphs, addition of new information and contextualization) can also be widely observed. In this respect, there is evidence that additional information is often obtained from other news texts circulated either through the webpage or in the newswire and that the practice of using several source texts is widespread. On the other hand, translated texts are typically reduced to about two-thirds of their original length, and the inverted pyramid structure clearly facilitates translation work as it is often the last paragraphs that are left out. Like in our former sample of AFP texts, in some cases texts have been tailored for their new markets by reorganizing information and emphasizing a different news angle, which is considered more relevant in the new context.

Analysing Reuters' textual output on the website allows for the comparison of same-language texts made available on different sites and targeted to specific publics. In the case of English, often very similar or almost exact versions are found on Reuters' UK and US websites. Of the ten news stories selected, eight appeared in both, one only in the British site and one only in the American. Most often, both sites offer very similar versions of texts, with only slight changes of spelling and minimal adaptations such as conversion of currencies or specification of nationality (e.g. 'Marines' in the US version and 'US Marines' in the British version). In some texts, slight modifications of title and the omission or alteration of sentences and short paragraphs can also be observed.

However, in the case of Spanish, practices differ completely. Not only do the Latin American and Spanish websites operate with complete autonomy from each other, privileging the news that is of more relevance to their specific regions, they also each translate from English to suit their own particular needs. This means that often two different Spanish translations of articles originally written in English are available. This is true of four of the ten texts found in translation for 20 July 2006, which appeared in both the Latin American and the Spanish websites.

The fact that often two different Spanish translations from the same text exist might seem to point to an unnecessary duplication of effort and needs to be examined in some detail. One of the four examples available in our selection of texts is an article entitled 'Israeli troops battle Hizbollah inside Lebanon', which has been rendered as 'Israel se enfrenta a Hezbolá en Líbano, Annan pide alto el fuego' (Spain's website) and 'RESUMEN – Tropas Israel luchan contra Hizbollah dentro del Líbano' (Latin America's website). The latter text follows the English version closely, narrating in roughly the same order the confrontations between Israeli troops and Hizbollah guerrillas in Lebanon and the reported number of victims on both sides, Kofi Annan's call for an immediate end to hostilities, the deployment of a small US force of Marines to evacuate American citizens to neigh-bouring Cyprus, the position of the Israeli government, the possibility of a ground offensive and Israel's attacks in the Gaza strip. Only four paragraphs (dealing with the evacuations by US Marines and Israel's promise to let aid into Lebanon) towards the end are eliminated. By contrast, the (shorter) version available in Spain's website consistently rewrites the original text, eliminating about one-half of its contents, adding new information possibly extracted from another article and substantially reorganizing paragraphs. While informing on the confrontations and number of victims on each side and adding direct quotes from both Israeli and Hizbollah sources, this version omits the description of the evacuation of American citizens, which is merely summarized in its last paragraph, and foregrounds Annan's plea for a ceasefire (as is evident in its title) and possible diplomatic negotiations in this direction.

Such a change of informative angle is already evident in the translation of the first paragraph or lead, which summarizes the whole text and gives its most essential facts. Source text:

Hizbollah fought fierce battles with Israeli troops on the Lebanese border on Thursday, as thousands more foreigners fled the nine-day-old war in Lebanon, including 1,000 Americans evacuated by US Marines.

Version 1 (Latin America):

Hizbollah sostuvo el jueves fieros enfrentamientos contra tropas israelíes en la frontera libanesa, mientras miles de extranjeros huían de Beirut debido a la guerra que se ha extendido por nueve días.

(Hizbollah fought fierce battles with Israeli troops on the Lebanese border on Thursday, as thousands of foreigners fled Beirut due to the nine-day-old war.)

Version 2 (Spain):

Israel mantuvo el jueves fuertes enfrentamientos militares con Hezbolá en la frontera libanesa, mientras el secretario general de Naciones Unidas, Kofi Annan, pidió un cese inmediato de las hostilidades.

(Israel fought fierce military battles with Hizbollah on the Lebanese border on Thursday, as secretary general of the United Nations, Kofi Annan, demanded an immediate cease to hostilities.)

Both translations preserve the author's signature, but offer significantly different versions of the original English text and can no longer be approached as mere duplications of information, but need to be seen as specific texts adapted to singular contexts which emphasize the facts that are considered most relevant in each case.

The two French translations in the sample follow the example of the second Spanish version, considerably changing and rewriting the original source texts. Thus, the above text was also made available in the French website, entitled 'Diplomatie et évacuations profitent d'une pause', with the following lead:

Les raids de l'aviation israélienne au Liban ont marqué une pause relative qui a favorisé les évacuations d'étrangers, rendu plus audibles les appels à l'arrêt des hostilités et entrouvert un espace à la diplomatie.

(Israeli air raids in Lebanon have relatively halted aiding the evacuation of foreigners, rendering appeals for a cease to hostilities louder and opening up a space for diplomacy.)

Like Spanish version 2, this text focusses on Annan's call for a ceasefire and omits describing the evacuations of American citizens under way. Notably, it gives details of Israel's attack against Hizbollah's chief, Hassan Nasrallah, also quoting the latter from an interview aired by Al-Jazeera (to which the Spanish version also refers). In the French text, Nasrallah's views are given more prominence and emphasized under a new subtitle ('Nasrallah nie tout affaiblissement'). This text also goes with more detail into the specific measures proposed by Annan, while mentioning the ongoing evacuations to Cyprus (and specifically those involving French citizens) at its end. The French text only shares about one-third of its content with the original English version, although it is of a similar length, pointing to the fact that, through translation, significantly different versions of texts are globally circulated. One single organization, such as Reuters, bears witness to this widespread profusion of interconnected texts.

Contraflow in global news: IPS' coverage of the World Social Forum

The last study in this chapter focusses on articles, and their translations, produced by Inter Press Service in its coverage of the World Social Forum 2004, which took place in Mumbai from 16 to 21 January. By sampling all the articles (and their translations) produced about a single event a more quantitative element is introduced into this textual analysis of agency news. Thus, rather than exploring and comparing specific texts and their translations, this section will deal more generally with issues concerning IPS' coverage of the event as a whole, with a specific emphasis on language and translation. The main differences between IPS and other agencies' textual output have been explained in the last chapter. As we have seen, IPS produces longer articles of a more analytical nature, with the aim to offer an in-depth look at the issues described. With respect to translation, the organization's global services translate between English and Spanish in both directions, while networks in a number of European and Third World countries ensure that news can also be made available in fourteen other languages.

IPS focusses on global events from the perspective of civil society and the South. The World Social Forum, which since 2001 has gathered representatives of civil society to discuss global problems and possibilities for alternative development, is clearly a very important event for the organization in terms of news relevance, covered widely in its website and also in its daily paper *TerraViva* during the course of the meetings. It is also worthwhile noting that questions of language and translation have been explicitly raised at the Social Forums, leading to the creation of an international network of volunteer interpreters and translators, Babels, which describes itself as a player in the anti-capitalist debate. According to its Charter, among the objectives of Babels are to affirm the right of everybody to express themselves in the language of their choice and to contribute to discussions on the part language plays in the mechanisms of cultural domination and in the circulation of ideas between the various social and citizens' movements.

These issues are clearly relevant in the World Social Forum, where representatives of countries from all over the world meet. The Mumbai 2004 edition was the first to be held outside Latin America, which posed new questions and difficulties regarding language use and communication between the different cultural groups.

Like Reuters, IPS privileged the internet early on as a medium for communicating its news directly to the public. In its webpage most news stories are freely available, while access to restricted items requires the introduction of a password by clients. The outlook of the various websites, currently available in thirteen languages (English, Spanish, French, Swedish, Italian, German, Turkish, Swahili, Dutch, Arabic, Finnish, Portuguese and Japanese), is very similar. The most relevant news stories are found at its centre, while columns on the right provide links to other top news and to highlighted themes. On the left-hand side, links to sub-pages in which news is classified according to region (Global Affairs, Africa, Asia-Pacific, Caribbean, Europe, Latin America, Mideast and Mediterranean, North America) or theme (Development, Civil Society, Globalization, Environment, Human Rights, Health, Indigenous Peoples, Economy and Trade, Labour, Population, Arts and Entertainment) appear. Abstracts of weekly columns (shorter texts by distinguished commentators who are members of IPS' columnist service) directed at subscribing media organizations are also made available.

For this study IPS' English, Spanish, French and Dutch websites were consulted. The French website, however, only offers African news of a regional character, and did not contain any articles related to the World Social Forum (WSF). Therefore the sample is based on articles from three websites in the two global services of the organization (Spanish and English) and in a European minority language (Dutch). The first thing to be noticed is that in all these websites, and in contrast with mainstream news organizations, coverage was not limited to the six days in which the WSF took place (16–21 January), but started gradually as far as eight days before the meeting was due to begin, finishing one day after its end. Coverage intensified three days before the beginning of the event, and was maintained (except at the weekend) with a similar degree of intensity until its end. During this time, the three websites offered at least one new article, but often two or more, every day on issues related to the WSF (see Table 6.1).

Table 6.1 Number of articles published by language (January 2004).

	Thurs 8	Fri 9	Sat 10	Sun 11	Mon 12	Tues 13	Wed 14	Thurs 15	**Fri 16**	**Sat 17**	**Sun 18**	**Mon 19**	**Tues 20**	**Wed 21**	Thurs 22	Total
English		1			2	3	1	3	1	1		3	2	1	1	19
Spanish	1				1	1	2	2	2	1		2	5	1	1	19
Dutch				1		4	1	1	3		1	4	2	3	1	21
Total	1	1	0	1	3	8	4	6	6	2	1	9	9	5	3	59

Note: dates in bold are when the World Social Forum (WSF) took place.

A total number of 59 texts, including original articles and translations, were published on the three websites. An equal number appeared in English and Spanish (19), while the Dutch website offered two more articles than the other two websites. This high number can easily be explained with reference to the type of text published: more than 60 per cent of the articles published in the Dutch website are translations (see Table 6.2).

The fourth edition of the WSF, described as 'an annual gathering of non-governmental groups and activists critical of the current world economic and political order', was the first to be held outside Porto Alegre (Brazil), which had housed the event since 2001. The 12 articles and their translations (a total of 24 articles or 40.6 per cent of all texts related to the WSF) that appeared before the actual start of the event introduce issues that are specific to this edition of the event, pointing to its celebration in Mumbai as an important step in making 'the global gathering truly global', and specifying that a high level of local participation is expected, including a high number of poor people. They also give profiles of a city characterized by sharp social contrasts in the context of neo-liberal globalization, statistics of WSF participants and current criticisms of the initiative, including the organization of a parallel forum called Mumbai Resistance 2004. A number of these articles, written by IPS stringers from their respective regions (New Delhi, Rio de Janeiro, Bangkok, Brussels, Nairobi), deal especially with regional aspects related to the organization of the forum and with the participation of activists from different nationalities: among them, the celebration of local fora in Belgium; the housing problem in Nairobi, which is due to be raised by Kenyan activists in Mumbai; the description of a Thai factory owned by its workers, who organize a workshop at the WSF; the assistance of Pakistani delegates, and the difficulties of attendance for poorer Latin American activists.

From 13 January, contributions datelined in Mumbai start to appear: they account for 20 of the 31 original articles dedicated to the event. In addition to some casual collaborations, several IPS correspondents cover the forum in Mumbai: Marwaan Macan-Markar and Ranjit Devraj in English; Raúl Pierri and Mario Osava in Spanish; Gie Goris in Dutch. Articles produced from the start of the event (19 originals and their translations) chronicle its development, focussing on points as diverse as the poor slums just outside the gates of the WSF, the organization of global peace and anti-Bush demonstrations on the first anniversary of the invasion of Iraq, the recuperation of the diversity of rice seeds in Asia, and African countries' need to stop paying debt. Coverage also deals with seminars and workshops dedicated to themes such as international organizations and civil society, and globalization and security, and with the contributions of well-known figures like Joseph Stiglitz, Mary Robinson, Nawal el Saadawi and Federico Mayor Zaragoza. Underlying issues such as the increased diversity of participants, criticisms of the WSF and reflections on the future of the gathering are specially dealt with in the five articles which from 20 January start summing up and evaluating the event.

As indicated above, translations account for the high number of texts published on the Dutch website (13 out of 21 texts, or 61.9 per cent). On the English and Spanish websites, this proportion is inverted, but the number of translated texts is still remarkably high at around 40 per cent (see Table 6.2). In total, translations amount to nearly one-half of all articles circulated (28).

We can certainly gain a sense of what contraflow in global news and an alternative politics of language and translation mean by examining the direction of translation. In the former analysis of Reuters' website, translation emanated exclusively from English into other languages. Here the outlook is very different: although 16 of the 28 translations in the sample are from an English original, 12 have a Spanish source text. 11 of the 12 original English texts were translated and made available in other websites; most of them (6) in both Spanish and Dutch news services. 7 of the 11 original Spanish texts were translated into other languages, including 5 texts which were translated for both the English and the Dutch sites. As IPS' global translation services only operate between English and Spanish, none of the 8 original Dutch texts was translated, which thus remained limited to the local Dutch service.

The important role played by translation facilitated a more inclusive coverage of the WSF activities, a coverage that does not emanate exclusively from a single-language or cultural outlook and which incorporates information obtained in different languages and available, for this reason, to journalists with different linguistic competencies. IPS' news translation follows the procedures that are more generally associated with news translation (abundant rewriting and reorganizing, possibility to eliminate and add information) with one significant difference from the other news agencies: translators tend to have more time to do their job, which is reflected in the fact that translated texts often appear on the website one day after the originals.

Table 6.2 Number of original articles and translations by language.

	Original texts			Translations	Total
	Total no.		Translated into		
English (Eng)	12	11	Sp+D 6 Sp 2 D 3	7	19
Spanish (Sp)	11	7	Eng+D 5 Eng 2 D 0	8	19
Dutch (D)	8	0		13	21
Total	31			28	59

Nowhere is the importance of translation more remarkable than on the Dutch website, which is translated locally. This not only contained a higher number of translated texts than the other two websites, but in them a much higher degree of rewriting and transformation of original texts could also be observed. Most Dutch translations were heavily summarized and rewritten, incorporating new details considered of interest to the Belgian Dutch-speaking public. In this way, translations ideally complemented the excellent coverage from Belgium (including news on a local social forum in Mechelen, on Belgian participants in the WSF and on celebrations organized in a Belgian village called Bombaye) and Mumbai in Dutch, which centred on issues of local interest. The high degree of rewriting in the Dutch transla-tions leads on several occasions to the modification of the byline or authorial credit of texts. In one case, an article which was a summary of two source texts (one in Spanish and one in English) appeared under the name of both authors. Most significantly, on two occasions the translator appeared as co-author, inaugurating an unusually active and explicitly recognized role of the translator as author. In the first case, a text dealing with Bernard Cassen's criticisms of the WSF, the rewriter added about 40 per cent of new text to refer to the opinions of other distinguished European participants. The second text, describing Joseph Stiglitz's intervention at the WSF, is a com-pletely different version produced by a journalist who was present at the panel, and who also used some information provided by a Spanish-language article on the same subject. Classifying these texts as originals or translations is to a certain extent arbitrary,[2] pointing to the hybrid nature of practices which have resulted from an alternative politics of language that promotes the visibility of translation.

Conclusion

Journalistic texts are written for specific audiences, according to the princi-ples of news relevance and background knowledge of the target reader. Existing networks of foreign correspondents, which gather news from around the world for one particular news organization, are based on this need to design news texts for their audiences which are always divided along geo-graphical, socio-cultural and linguistic lines. In Chapter 4, we saw that news agencies have developed their own specific dual structures, through which information is produced in several languages (typically at least a local lan-guage and the international language used globally by the organization) at the same time, to respond to this requirement. However, the generation of a myriad of texts in different languages specifically tailored for a wide range of audiences is practically impossible, and translation appears in this context as the second best option to respond to the different needs of publics world-wide. In the absence of an original, news translation intervenes to rewrite a text for a new public, a text which is specifically redesigned for the target reader and which often resembles a new text rather than a translation. We have shown how alterations of the order of paragraphs, contextualization and addition of new information, elimination of paragraphs that are no longer considered relevant and even the privileging of different news angles are all part of the ordinary operations of news translation.

In order to understand the role of news translation it is necessary to consider the unequal distribution of power and, in particular, the directionality of translation flows in the market of global news. Western news organizations have dominated the journalistic field since its inception, creating the very structures and networks that made the existence of a global communications system possible. This has meant that certain European languages have predominated and, in the past decades, that English has become the most global of the global languages. Although language and translation have not been an explicit issue in the ongoing debate around the Western dominance of global news channels that was inaugurated in the 1970s by UNESCO, they express global inequalities directly and their examination contributes to an understanding of the mechanisms of global dominance in the field of news.

Language and translation are of central importance in order to grasp how news flows shape global and local contexts. Translation enables texts to travel to new contexts, overcoming linguistic and cultural boundaries, and making them truly global, i.e. able to speak to audiences that are divided by cultural and linguistic boundaries. Texts are shaped by news values which have been globalized by the Western news organizations, as well as by the local context in which they are produced. This means that, to a certain degree, translation is facilitated between news markets that have all accommodated to common norms and values of objectivity, neutrality, newsworthiness, etc. In addition, a high degree of domestication and transparency are the norm for adapting texts to new contexts, in which culturally specific features are removed or modified in such a way that translations, often resembling new texts, are able to respond to the information needs of new audiences. In this context, the necessary discussion of whether it is ultimately Western news values and worldviews that are transmitted cannot be answered by reference to language and translation alone, and is ultimately related to the globalization of Western communication networks and media practices and to the continued predominance of Western news organizations, which are only challenged by alternative practices and organizations such as IPS and Babels.

Translation has been incorporated into the process of news production of the global news agencies to ensure that texts reach their main news markets at the greatest speed and with maximum efficiency. However, like the agencies themselves, whose important role in the field of global news is not always apparent, translation has remained invisible. Recently, the internet has increased the visibility of agency texts with the general public, while also generating new information needs and a greater demand for local information. News agencies have responded with the creation of new customized and multimedia online products characterized by their high flexibility and adaptation to clients' needs and also, significantly, by the production of their own websites in a variety of localized versions, which also multiply the visibility of translated texts. Studying how translation intervenes at the textual level reveals the conditions, norms and practices governing the production of these texts and helps to explain its crucial role in the field of global news.

7   Translation and trust

Truthfulness and news reporting

In our world of mass communication, of ever-increasing speed, our world of twenty-four-hour breaking news, where text messages can be sent from scenes of disaster even as politicians are issuing statements denying that the disaster has happened, the one certain thing that we all cling to is the importance of the truthfulness of news reporters. We need to believe in the veracity of the accounts provided by those men and women around the world who supply us with information about the events that shape our lives, and when such information is proven to be false, we are outraged. In 2004, the editor of a national British newspaper was forced to resign when he authorized the publication of photographs, purporting to show British soldiers abusing prisoners in Iraq, that turned out to be fakes. In such a situation, we all feel abused. In those countries where governments interfere with the freedom of the press, we are equally outraged, for press freedom and truthfulness go hand in hand.

A fundamental premise in the transmission of news is that it should be truthful. The assumption of a reader of a newspaper or a viewer switching on the television to watch the evening news is that whatever is reported will be relayed to them honestly. Yet, as has been discussed earlier in this book, the processes whereby a news item comes into being and is realized in print or visual form are multiple, complex and manipulative. The end product that is read or seen has been shaped for its receivers, mediated through several sets of filters that are determined by time or space constraints, editorial policy, cultural acceptability and a host of other factors that have been examined in previous chapters. Moreover, the multiplicity is accentuated when the news is transposed interlingually at some point in the process, and here we encounter the additional problem that bedevils discourse about translation, that is, the extent to which any translation can be said to be a truthful, accurate rendering of a source text.

In Chapter 1 it was shown that from the perspective of translation analysis, *skopos* theory is one of the most useful approaches, because it is premised on a notion of equivalent effect, not on any notion of exact textual transference. *Skopos* theory serves us well as a starting point for a discussion of news translation, but has its limitations when we start to compare the way in which the same translated news story is presented in different newspapers. The enormous divergence of presentational aspects takes us beyond the interlingual into other aspects of textual manipulation that prevail in the target culture.

Here ideological constraints come to the fore, and as Alberto Orengo has shown in an essay on Italian newspapers, it might be more helpful to adopt a theory of 'localization' when examining how a news item is shaped for what he calls 'sub-locales' (Orengo, 2005).

One of the principal difficulties in analysing news translation is that not only are there different conventions operating in different countries, but within each country there are huge divergencies of style and expectations that are both market and politically driven. Yet at the same time there are common threads that can be discerned in the way in which a story is presented, and this commonality may well be driven by accessibility to shared visual images, rather than to any common verbal elements.

Let us consider, for example, different treatments of the capture and trial of Saddam Hussein in certain British, French and Italian newspapers, starting with the first images of the ousted dictator after his capture in December 2003. Saddam had gone into hiding when the Allied troops defeated his loyal forces, but was finally tracked down. As the war in Iraq degenerated into what many saw as an occupation, with the level of violence in everyday life spiralling out of any government's control, the capture of the man deemed responsible for it all was bound to be of great significance. Media coverage of the event was extensive and visually very graphic. Saddam had been found in a rough hideout and the first images transmitted showed an elderly man with unkempt hair and beard, very different from the images of the powerful figure in military uniform commanding an army and ruling a state.

One particularly striking photograph showed him undergoing an intrusive dental examination immediately after his arrest. This degrading image held various connotations: it emphasized his fall from a high position to his present powerlessness, it hinted that he had been reduced to a level little more than an animal, yet conversely it also implied that his captors were humane people, sufficiently concerned about his welfare to subject him to a medical examination. The image served, then, to stress the abjectness of Saddam Hussein along with the implicit suggestion that he was being well-cared for by his captors. The foregrounding of this image became a narrative in itself, setting the tone for what was to follow. In the case of the coverage of Saddam Hussein's trial, as we shall see later, there was a systematic use of visual images to offset the verbal.

Some months after the abject images were broadcast around the world, Saddam made his first appearance in court. Reports from diverse countries stressed how different he now looked, with his hair and beard trimmed and wearing clean clothes. Reporting that first court appearance prior to the trial proper, the *Daily Telegraph* on 2 July 2004 carried a half-page photograph of Saddam, smartly dressed in a pinstriped jacket and open-necked white shirt, raising a finger in the air as he speaks to the court. Above the photograph is a headline that states 'Defiant and finger-wagging, Saddam the deposed dictator faces justice at last.' The cover story tells us that he looks slimmer and healthier than when last seen, and that he was wearing 'a grey pinstriped jacket, brown trousers and shiny black shoes'.

Clothes featured prominently in many of the accounts of the start of the trial and this seems to be an example of a cross-cultural thread that was developed to a greater or lesser extent in all three national press systems. The *Corriere della sera* story on the first day of the trial, 19 October 2005, carried a headline that focussed on his appearance, 'Vestito scuro e il Corano tra le mani' (Dark suit and the Koran in his hand), and the subsequent feature zooms in on the physical appearance of the deposed dictator. The dark suit denotes elegance and sobriety, the Koran is presented here as a prop to reinforce his image of refinement and sincerity. *Le Figaro* on the same date goes into even more detail:

> Vêtu d'un costume sombre, le col de sa chemise blanche ouvert, Saddam Hussein, les cheveux mi-longs mais soigneusement teints, la barbe poivre et sel et les traits tirés, fait ses 68 ans.

> (Wearing a dark suit, his white shirt open-necked, his hair longish but expertly dyed, with his salt and pepper beard and his face drawn, Saddam Hussein looked all of his 68 years.)

The phrase 'soigneusement teints' implies vanity, for although his hair is still slightly long ('mi-longs') he has ensured that the streaks of white so prominent in the capture images have been removed. *The Times* even carried a story on 30 November about Saddam's tailor, Recep Cesur, apparently a Kurd from Istanbul. Cesur, we are informed, 'has become the style guru to the Middle East', and used to supply the former dictator with fifty new suits every second month. The entire Iraqi cabinet along with the Iraqi football team were dressed by Cesur. After Saddam's arrest, Cesur was summoned to measure him again and then made four new suits for the much thinner man. Saddam's clothes became headline news, with even his tailor featured as the subject of an article. Saddam's appearance in court at the start of his trial was explicitly contrasted with the last images of him that had gone round the world, images of a tired old man, his mouth open for the dentist's probe, with untrimmed beard and feral hair. The clothing theme cannot be traced to a single source, so cannot be said to have been directly translated, but it surfaced repeatedly as trope, as a common means of signalling to readers that there was a gap between appearances and reality besides being used as an instrument of ridicule.

What these stories also show is a first stage in what was to develop into the theatricalization of a sensational trial. When Saddam was first captured, the front page of the tabloid newspaper the *Sun* prefigured that theatricalization in its layout. Almost two-thirds of the page was given over to a photograph of the unkempt, staring-eyed newly captured dictator, with a small image down in the lower left-hand corner of a dapper Saddam's head and shoulders. Alongside the name of the paper were two words in block capitals: 'SADDAM CAPTURED'. The main headline, which took up almost the whole of the left-hand side of the page facing the photograph, was the phrase 'WE GOT HIM'. Just above was the familiar public address phrase of 'Ladies and gentlemen...', which served to introduce the dramatic headline. 'WE GOT HIM' became 'Ladies and gentlemen, we got him', a rhetorical device which created a slightly comic tone. The *Sun* was therefore effectively presenting Saddam Hussein to the public, just as the old music-hall presenters would introduce the next act.

Determining sincerity

In an essay that looks at media coverage in the aftermath of the death of Princess Diana on 31 August 1997, Martin Montgomery discusses ways in which audiences constructed their own ideas about the sincerity of what they saw and heard on radio and television. The essay examines ways in which members of the British public reacted to the three highest-profile tributes broadcast by the BBC in the days following Diana's death. The first of these was a television interview given by Tony Blair barely six hours after news of the Paris crash had reached him, when he invented the term 'the people's princess' that was to become enshrined in the reporting of the death around the world. Standing in the open air, surrounded by microphones, the British Prime Minister spoke without notes direct to camera, his voice trembling and hesitant with emotion.

On 5 September came the second major broadcast, a speech to the nation by the Queen, broadcast from Buckingham Palace, in which she expressed her sadness at the death of her daughter-in-law and declared that she was speaking as 'your Queen and as a grandmother'. This broadcast was made live, using a teleprompter and showed the Queen composed and speaking clearly and fluently. The third speech analysed was the address by Diana's brother, the Earl Spencer, at her funeral service in Westminster Abbey, when he pledged that her 'blood family' would do all they could to raise her sons as she would have wished and appeared to be on the verge of breaking down in tears towards the end of his oration.

Montgomery carefully examines these three broadcasts, noting rhetorical devices such as hyperbole, patterns of repetition, pairings ('your Queen and a grandmother') but above all analysing patterns of intonation and body language. The fundamental question he addresses is how does an audience identify and judge the sincerity of a speaker, and in investigating this he examines a range of responses to all three speeches. More generally, he notes that some speech acts may project an impression of sincerity far more than others:

Speech acts such as complimenting, apologizing and promising may be seen as *routinely* implicating sincerity. But speech acts such as commanding, requesting, passing sentence and excommunicating do not. A judge, for instance, may direct a trial jury to acquit but has to pass sentence on a defendant if a guilty verdict is reached: the sentence will be passed effectively, irrespective of the judge's emotional commitment to it. Promising, on the other hand, includes sincerity as a condition of its satisfactory performance.

(Montgomery, 1999: 21)

With these criteria in mind, he argues that although the three speeches were all, in different ways, received as 'sincere', it was the performance of Diana's brother, which included marked signs of personal emotion, that was seen as most sincere, while the Queen's more measured broadcast was assessed more negatively, probably because of her emotional understatement and more formal presentation. Montgomery points out that the way in which speech acts are framed and presented conditions how we respond to what is said: the human significance of speech resides 'not just in the way it means something propositionally in the here and now, but also in the ways it can be deemed valid (or invalid) in the here and now' (Montgomery, 1999: 12).

Montgomery's theoretical starting point is Habermas' discussion of validity claims. Habermas suggests that the validity of speech will depend on judgements of its truth, appropriateness or sincerity, but whereas truth and appropriateness will be valued through negotiation in the discourse, sincerity has to be taken on trust and validated by the speaker's behaviour. Following Habermas, Montgomery argues that speech in the public sphere projects itself as valid by being perceived as true, sincere or appropriate, or as one or other of these three.

In a later essay, he develops these ideas and focusses on what he terms 'authentic talk' in the public sphere, noting, however, that broadcast talk is normally staged for performance in some way. His conclusion is interesting: he suggests that it is neither the authority of the speaker nor any sense of a source being somehow 'authorized' that will determine whether a broadcast will be perceived as truthful, but rather it is 'the nature and the manner of the talk itself that makes for compelling testimony' (Montgomery, 2001: 404). In other words, the validity of a speech act will be assessed according to diverse sign systems and to the contexts in which it is made and received. In the case of the tributes to Diana, the fact that one speech was made in the immediate aftermath of her death by a senior politician and another at her funeral by her brother appeared to convey a greater sense of validation than the more formal broadcast by the Queen which came after several days of intense media speculation about silence from Buckingham Palace. This was despite the language of the Queen's speech which contained sentences such as 'I say from my heart' and 'I admired and respected her'. What this shows is that assessments of authenticity are both subjective and conditioned by context as well as by body language, intonation and choice of vocabulary.

Theatricalizing the news

Actors, of course, understand this well, and manipulate responses accordingly, but the difference between a broadcast news interview and a piece of theatre is that the former is deemed to be more authentic because more spontaneous while the latter only conveys a sense of authenticity in a situation that everyone knows to be contrived. Despite this obvious difference, the tools for analysing broadcast news as demonstrated by Montgomery and those for analysing performance are very similar, as both in their different ways are complex semiotic systems that audiences then have to decode.

When interviews, conversations or more formal exchanges such as parliamentary debates or courtroom scenes are transcribed and published, however, issues of veracity and authenticity become more fuzzy, for the physical dimension is removed. When we read an interview in a newspaper we do not have access to the body language, the changes of tone of voice, the pace of the conversation or the original context. Nevertheless, Habermas' tripartite distinction between truth, appropriateness and sincerity can still serve when we examine such texts, particularly when there is substantial use of direct quotes or when an exchange is laid out as though it were a dramatic work, with the names of speakers given before each utterance. In such cases what takes place is a process of theatricalization, with a real-life exchange being written up as though it were a piece of theatre. This strategy, which is not very common, raises important questions about the assessment of veracity, given the point made above about theatre itself being perceived as intrinsically less authentic than news reporting. When a newspaper chooses to set down an event in the form of a dramatic text it deserves critical attention, since this would seem to be a strategy utilized for a particular end. In some cases, the interview may be accompanied by an article effectively commenting on it, but at other times the dramatic text format may stand alone to be read like a play. The dramatic text layout was used frequently in the reporting of the trial of Saddam Hussein as we shall see shortly.

Veracity and domestication

In the opening chapter of this book, we noted the impossibility of exact translation across any languages. No translation can ever reproduce in identical format something that has been written in another language, since no two languages have identical semantic and syntactic patterns. One of the passages cited above, in *Le Figaro*, for example, contains the phrase 'Saddam Hussein ... fait ses 68 ans'. This is an idiomatic expression that translates into English as 'looked all of his 68 years', a phrase that has equivalent effect according to Vermeer's *skopos* model, but is by no means an exact-word-for-word translation of the French. Variation is an inevitable aspect of translation, but the question that is always present is whether there is a limit to the extent of possible variation. If variation is so extreme that there is no trace of a source text, can this still be said to be translation? This question lies at the heart of any discussion of news translation, where often the only traceable source is an event, and not any single identifiable textual account of that event. Yet clearly, given the way in which news is gathered, what tends to happen is that the source material is synthesized even as it is transferred across languages, then adjusted stylistically in accordance with target culture norms.

The question both of definitions of translation and of the veracity of translated accounts was particularly apparent in the reporting in the British press of the first court appearance of Saddam Hussein in July 2004. Alongside accounts of the event some of the British papers also carried transcripts of the relatively brief appearance of the former Iraqi dictator before a judge, again a curiously theatrical gesture. We can assume that the intention of publishing transcripts was to convey a heightened sense of veracity, inviting readers to believe that what they were reading was a straightforward, unadulterated account of what had happened in the courtroom. At the same time, though, given the theatricalization of the whole process from the moment of publication of the first images of him after his capture, the publication of transcripts also served to enhance the soap opera effect of the reportage. Indeed, in the *Daily Telegraph* the theatrical dimension was highlighted, when the report stated that 'Saddam was not going to leave the stage without saying his piece'. The trial was being constructed in the media as a piece of global theatre.

What is particularly interesting is that the published transcripts, though all purporting to be accurate translations of an original, were surprisingly different. The *Independent* reminded readers that the transcript was incomplete in that it had been edited, but then added the curious note that some parts of the conversation were not included in the original transcript at all:

> The following is an edited transcript of the translators' words as Saddam Hussein answered questions from judge Ra'id Juhi. Some parts of the conversation were not included in the original transcript.
>
> (Independent, 2nd July 2004)

What this statement seems to be saying is that during the hearing journalists were producing their own versions of what was being said and that when it was over, their texts were amalgamated with an official transcript, which did not contain all the exchanges recorded collectively. The online version of this article notes that the microphone did not pick up everything. Whether this is what happened, however, can only be surmised.

The *Daily Telegraph* also published what was described as a 'transcript', but added a sentence by way of a preface stating, 'Saddam's courtroom exchanges with the judge yesterday included', thereby signalling that what was being reproduced was a pared-down edited version. The *Daily*

Telegraph version was considerably shorter than the one published in the *Independent*.

In considering these two published transcripts, the question that they raise concerns both trust and veracity. Readers unable to access an original Arabic version have to rely on what they read in English as offering an accurate, truthful version of what took place in the courtroom. Yet even a cursory reading of the two versions shows some significant differences. In the *Independent* the transcript opens with a sentence that serves as a kind of stage direction: 'The judge opened proceedings by asking Saddam for his name.' This is what follows:

> SADDAM: ... Hussein Majid, the president of the Republic of Iraq.
> The judge then asks his date of birth.
> SADDAM: 1937.
> JUDGE: Profession? Former president of the Republic of Iraq?
> SADDAM: No, present. Current. It's the will of the people.
> JUDGE: The head of the Baath Party that is dissolved, defunct. Former commander and chief of the army. Residence is Iraq. Your mother's name?
> SADDAM: Sobha. You also have to introduce yourself to me.
> JUDGE: Mr Saddam, I am the investigative judge of the central court of Iraq.
> SADDAM: So that I have to know, you are an investigative judge of the central court of Iraq? What resolution, what law formed this court?
> The judge's response could not be heard.
>
> (*Independent*, 2 July 2004)

The version in the *Telegraph* also contains stage directions. In the extract reprinted here, the stage direction is in the form of a movement on the part of the judge, but later in the transcript Saddam speaks 'as he is led away by guards'. The effect of these pseudo stage directions is to give the scene a vitality and to suggest something of the body language and kinesics that would have been evident to people present in the courtroom. But the linguistic register of the *Telegraph* version is different, and the speech acts reproduced are also different. If we compare the two versions, we can grasp the gist of the exchanges between Saddam and the judge, but little else:

> JUDGE: Are you the former president of Iraq?
> SADDAM: I am Saddam Hussein, president of Iraq.
> JUDGE (to court clerk): Put down 'former' in brackets.
> SADDAM: I am the president of the republic so you should not strip me of my title to put me on trial.
> JUDGE: You are the ex-leader of Iraq and the ex-leader of the dissolved armed forces. Were you the leader of the Ba'ath party and head of the armed forces?
> SADDAM: Yes. I've introduced myself to you but you haven't introduced yourself to me. So who are you?

JUDGE: I am a judge of the criminal courts of Iraq.

SADDAM: So you repress Iraqis under the orders of the coalition? Do you represent the American coalition?

(*Daily Telegraph*, 2 July 2004)

Both these versions have been edited, as is clearly stated, they differ in terms of information supplied, the structure of the questioning and responses, the choreography of the event (in one version we are told that the judge's reply cannot be heard, whilst the other version has the judge giving an instruction to the court clerk) and the tone. The judge in the first version comes across as a more authoritative figure. When he refers to Saddam's role as former chief of the army, he states this rather than putting it as a question which is the case in the second version. He also asks for the name of Saddam's mother, which is not recorded in the *Daily Telegraph*. The judge answers Saddam's question quite differently in each version: he claims to be variously the 'investigative judge of the central court of Iraq' and 'a judge of the criminal courts of Iraq'.

The differences between the two versions become more notable as we read on. Saddam makes much longer speeches in the *Independent*, and challenges the judge on several occasions. The charges are listed, which is not the case in the *Daily Telegraph*. At one stage in the *Daily Telegraph* version, Saddam is quoted as saying that when he gave orders for the invasion of Kuwait, he was 'looking out for Iraqi interests against those mad dogs who had tried to turn Iraqi women into 10-dinar prostitutes'. At this point the judge reprimands him and then asks him to sign a document listing his rights. This does not appear at all in the *Independent*, despite the fact that the *Independent* version is much longer.

The concluding exchange is also rather different. In the *Independent* Saddam refuses to sign any documents without his lawyers and the hearing ends with a robust exchange between the two parties:

SADDAM: Then please allow me not to sign anything until the lawyers are present.

JUDGE: That is fine. But this is your …

SADDAM: I speak for myself.

JUDGE: Yes, as a citizen you have the right. But the guarantees you have to sign because these were read to you, recited to you.

SADDAM: Anyway, why are you worried? I will come again before you with the presence of the lawyers, and you will be giving me all of these documents again. So why should we rush any action now and make mistakes because of rushed and hasty decisions or actions?

JUDGE: No, this is not a hasty decision-making now. I'm just investigating. And we need to conclude and seal the minutes.

SADDAM: No, I will sign when the lawyers are present.

JUDGE: Then you can leave.

    SADDAM: Finished?
    JUDGE: Yes.

In the *Daily Telegraph* the hearing ends differently:

    SADDAM: Would you accept if I do not sign this until the attendance of my lawyers?
    JUDGE: This is one of your rights.
    SADDAM: I am not interfering with your responsibilities.
    JUDGE: Fine, then let it be recorded that he has not signed. You are dismissed from the court.
    SADDAM: Finished?
    JUDGE: Finished.
    SADDAM (as he is led away by guards): Take it easy, I'm an old man.

Here there is no altercation, Saddam says very little before he is dismissed by the judge and a remark he apparently made to his guards is recorded as his final comment, a remark rendered into colloquial British English, a register that jars with the language he has been represented as using hitherto.

Do these details matter when both versions effectively give us the gist of what happened in the Iraqi court? The answer is that they do indeed matter, for once we as readers see the differences between what purport to be accurate, truthful versions of the same text the veracity of the reporting of the whole proceedings is called into question. From the perspective of a translation analyst, these differences also matter greatly, because the two texts create a very different impression of the event and, were they to be dramatized, actors would find themselves playing very different roles depending on which script they were given. The blustering, rather coarse man who emerges from the *Daily Telegraph* version is not the same as the more serious, articulate figure who argues a strong case in his own defence in the *Independent*. This version also has some awkward turns of phrase that suggest translationese and on the whole it sounds slightly more foreign than the other. A sentence attributed to Saddam such as 'I'm not holding fast to my position, but to respect the will of the people that decided to choose Saddam Hussein as leader of the revolution' is not a standard English construction. The retention of a degree of foreignness in the language serves both as a reminder to readers that the proceedings were not conducted in English and supplies a hint of Saddam's personal style of speaking. It also reinforces the idea of authenticity, and here the reputation of the *Independent* as a newspaper with a strong reporting tradition on Middle Eastern affairs and an editorial position opposed to the war in Iraq is a contributory factor in the process of representation of Saddam.

The *Daily Telegraph* version, in contrast, is a good example of a domesticated translation, where traces of foreignness in the language are played down or, as in the remark about 10-dinar prostitutes, inserted as local colour. The Saddam in this version is not so much a former dictator on the defensive, but a somewhat ridiculous figure, in contrast with the restrained urbanity of the judge who uses language that might be heard in an English court. These subtle textual differences lead readers in rather different directions. It is important to remember that domestication brings a text wholly into the target system, while the retention of foreign elements reminds readers that what they are encountering derives from somewhere else.

Returning to the issue of veracity, however, the question remains as to whether either of these texts can be considered a truthful translation of an existing transcript. Both are edited, and we are told that parts of the conversation reproduced in the longer version were not included in the original court transcript, though no indication of where those additions might have come from is given. The additions are nevertheless included as translations of verbatim material recorded somewhere by someone. We are left with a sense of uneasiness: if we have no Arabic, then we cannot check the accuracy or otherwise of either of these versions against any published transcript in the source language. All we have are two English translations of a composite transcript of a court hearing that took place in Arabic, both of which have been edited in different ways in conformity with the editorial policy of the different newspapers and the expectations of readers. We could say that a whole series of different processes of translation have taken place: from spoken to written, from Arabic to English, from full length to abbreviated, from initial copy to in-house style tailored for a particular readership, in one case following a strategy of domestication that is less evident in the other version. At every stage of those different processes, manipulations have taken place, though we are still invited to accept the final product as a true and accurate version for English readers.

Variations of veracity

The device of printing part of a court transcript diminished as the trial progressed, doubtless because of the extent of the material made available to the court, which required more summary and comment. The reproduction of transcripts served a purpose in the preliminary hearing and at the start of the trial, establishing what was to unfold in theatricalized terms. Several newspapers published excerpts from the court transcript on 20 October 2005, the day after Saddam made his first formal appearance at the start of the trial, but gradually supposedly verbatim exchanges gave way to articles written by journalists who were present in court. On 20 October the *Daily Telegraph* carried a short exchange between Saddam and the judge which it reported as an argument between the two men:

> JUDGE: Mr Saddam we ask you to write down your identity, your name, occupation and address and then we will allow you to talk. Now it is time to write down your identity.

SADDAM: I was not about to say much.

JUDGE: We want your identity, your name, and then we will listen to what you have. (*sic*) We are writing down the identities at this time. We will hear you when we need to listen to you.

SADDAM: First of all, who are you and what are you?

JUDGE: The Iraqi criminal court.

SADDAM: All of you are judges?

JUDGE: We don't have time to get into details. You can write down what you like.

SADDAM: I have been here in this military building since 2.30, and then from nine I have been wearing this suit. They have asked me to take it off and then put it on again many times.

JUDGE: Who are you? What is your identity? Why don't you take a seat and let the others say their names and we will get back to you.

SADDAM: You know me. You are an Iraqi and you know who I am. And you know I don't get tired.

JUDGE: These are formalities and we need to hear it from you.

SADDAM: They have prevented me from getting a pen and a paper because paper, it seems, is frightening these days. I don't hold any grudges against any of you. But upholding what is right and respecting the great Iraqi people who chose me I won't answer your questions or what you call a court, with all due respect to the individuals involved in it, and I reserve my constitutional rights as the president of Iraq. You know me.

JUDGE: There are the procedures. A judge cannot rely on personal knowledge.

SADDAM: I don't recognize the group that gave you the authority and assigned you. Aggression is illegitimate and what is built on illegitimacy is illegitimate.

The Italian newspaper *La Repubblica* carried a transcript on the same day, prefaced by the statement that there had been three hours of 'duello' (duelling) in the Baghdad court. In the Italian version, the judge, who is named as Judge Amin, asks Saddam to state his name, identity, status and profession. The verb 'communicare' is far more general than the English 'write down'. Then he explains that the court has set procedures which must be followed. At this point, Saddam interrupts:

SADDAM: Chi sei tu? Voglio sapere qual è il tuo ruolo.

GIUDICE AMIN: Noi siamo la corte penale irachena. Dunque, per cortesia, risponda: queste formalità non hanno nulla a che fare con lei.

SADDAM: Mi hanno fatto attendere per ore e non mi è stato concesso di portare carta e penna, perchè perfino le penne fanno paura oggi. (Saddam sorride.) Non nutro alcun risentimento per nessuno di voi. Ma mi rifaccio ai miei direitti e al rispetto che devo agli iracheni che mi hanno eletto. Non rispondo a questa cosidetta corte, con tutto il rispetto per chi ne fa parte. E mi riservo i diritti costituzionali di presidente della Repubblica dell'Iraq, non seguirò … Non riconosco nè l'entità che vi ha dato mandato e autorizzazione ne l'occupazione perchè tutto quello che e basato sulla falsità e falsità. … Hai mai fatto il giudice prima d'ora?

GIUDICE AMIN: Non c'e spazio per simili argomenti in questa Corte.

SADDAM: Sono in questa corte militare dalle 2 e mezzo di stanotte e dalle 9 del mattino son qui che vi aspetto con il mio vestito migliore. Tu sai chi sono, sento dal tuo accento che sei iracheno e dunque sai molto bene chi sono io, sai ch non mi stanco e non mi arrendo.

GIUDICE AMIN: Sono qui per chiedere formalmente della sua identità. Un giudice non può contare sulle proprie conoscenze personali.

SADDAM: Ho risposto a questa domanda per iscritto e te l'ho fatto avere.

(SADDAM: Who are you? I want to know what your role is.

JUDGE AMIN: We are the Iraqi penal court. So, please, answer: these formalities are nothing to do with you.

SADDAM: They kept me waiting for hours and I have not been allowed to bring paper and a pen with me, because even pens are frightening these days. (Saddam smiles.) I don't hold any grudges against any of you. But I insist on my rights and on the respect I owe to the Iraqi people who voted for me. I will not answer to this so-called court, with all respect to those who are involved in it. And I reserve my constitutional rights as president of the Iraqi republic, I will not go on … I recognize neither the body that gave you your mandate and authorization nor the occupation, because everything that is based on falsehood is false … Have you ever served as a judge before this?

JUDGE AMIN: There is no room for this kind of argument in this court.

SADDAM: I have been in this military court since half past two in the morning, and I have been waiting for you here in my best suit since nine am. You know who I am, I can tell from your accent that you are an Iraqi, so you know perfectly well who I am, you know I don't get tired and I don't give up.

JUDGE AMIN: I am here to ask you formally to declare your identity. A judge cannot rely on personal acquaintance.

SADDAM: I have replied to that question in writing and you have been given it.)

There are some significant differences between these two versions. The order of the exchanges is different, Saddam's complaints about being kept waiting and not being allowed paper and pen are in reverse order, in the Italian he says that he has been waiting in his best suit, while in the English version he complains that he has been required to dress and undress many times. In the Italian, he asks the judge whether has had previous experience, which does not appear in the English version, and he refers to the judge's Iraqi accent which is also omitted in English. Perhaps most significantly, in English he is credited with saying that aggression is illegitimate, while in Italian he speaks about 'falsità', falsehood and never talks about aggression, though he does refer to the occupation.

The relationship as it emerges from the language of the two men is also very different in English and Italian. Saddam uses the familiar 'tu' form, while the judge stays with the formal 'lei'. In Italian, the judge is courteous throughout the exchange, using phrases like 'per cortesia', while in English he is abrupt to the point of rudeness – 'You can write down what you like.'

The French newspaper *Le Figaro* published a partial transcript also on 20 October, under the headline 'Saddam Hussein defie ses juges'. In the introductory paragraph, we are told that the judge is Rizgar Mohammed Amin, of Kurdish origin. The first speech attributed to Saddam is 'Qui êtes-vous? Que me veut ce tribunal?' Here he uses the formal 'vous', which he does throughout, in contrast to the more intimate 'tu' in Italian which suggests disrespect on Saddam's part for the judge. The exchange reported in *Le Figaro* runs as follows:

'*Avez-vous déjà jugee auparavant?*' demande Saddam aux magistrates.

'*Monsieur Saddam, nous ne vous demandons pour l'instant que votre nom complet et votre profession*', retorque le juge, '*Vous aurez l'occasion de parler plus tard. Maintenant vous devez decliner votre identité, c'est une simple formalité.*'

Devant le refus de Saddam Hussein, le juge lit lui-même les noms et qualités de l'accusé. '*Saddam Hussein Majid, ancien président de l'Irak ... *'

'*Je ne dirais pas ancien président,*' l'interrompt Saddam, '*je dirais que je suis le président de la République irakienne.*'

'*Dites ce que vous voulez, mais pour moi ce n'est pas la même chose,*' lui retorque le juge, qui continue: '*commandant des forces armées. Résidence: Irak.*'

'*Vous me connaissez. Vous êtes irakien. Laissez-moi vous expliquer pourquoi je refuse de répondre à vos questions,*' le coupe Saddam. '*Je ne reconnais ni l'entité que vous à nomme, ni l'agression contre notre pays. Je me suis ici par respect pour le grand peuple irakien qui m'a choisi. Je demande que mes droits constitutionnels en tant que président de l'Irak soient reconnus. Cette cour n'est pas légale,*' dit il.

('Have you ever judged before?', Saddam asks the magistrate.

'Monsieur Saddam, all we are asking you for at this moment is your full name and your profession,' replies the judge. 'You will have an opportunity to speak later. Right now you should state your identity, this is a straightforward formality.'

When Saddam Hussein refuses, the judge reads out the name and details of the accused: 'Saddam Hussein Majid, former president of Iraq ... '

'I would not say former president,' Saddam interrupts. 'I would say that I am the president of the Iraqi Republic.'

'You may say what you like, but in my view that is not the same thing,' counters the judge, who goes on, 'commander of the armed forces. Resident in Iraq ... '

'You know me. You are an Iraqi. Allow me to explain why I refuse to answer your questions,' Saddam cuts in. 'I do not recognize the entity you have named, nor the aggression against our country. I am only here out of respect for the great Iraqi people who chose me. I demand that my constitutional rights as president of Iraq be recognized. This court is not legal,' he states.)

Here is yet another version with other significant differences, both in the order of the exchanges, in what is not there, compared with the English and Italian versions, and in how Saddam is presented. Since *Le Figaro* was always hostile to what it described right from the start as the American occupation of Iraq, it is not altogether surprising that Saddam should come across as a commanding figure, insisting on his constitutional rights and defying the court as an instrument of the occupying forces. By referring to his duty to the Iraqi people who chose him as their leader (the use of the verb 'choisir' is significant here, since it implies much more than an election, it suggest he is somehow the chosen one) Saddam comes across as more serious than in the other versions. The absurd almost caricature figure who emerges from the British press is light years away from the French presentation of a beleaguered statesman with a sense of moral dignity. But then, of course, France was opposed to the war in Iraq all along, while the British government allied itself to the Americans and demonizing Saddam was an essential part of the invasion propaganda machinery.

It is also the case that truth, appropriateness and sincerity are culturally determined, and are therefore variable. What passes as appropriate in one context may be deemed utterly inappropriate in another, but it is only through translation that such disparities emerge. The British use of irony and understatement would be highly inappropriate in a context where hyperbole and assertiveness are the norms. Part of the problem faced by journalists writing up the events of the Saddam Hussein trial derived from this disparity: some of his speeches in court, whilst acceptable in his own context, would have been read in a very different light had they remained unedited. The editing processes were therefore multi-layered, and involved recognizing differences in cultural expectations besides accommodating the house style and ideological position of the newspaper. At the same time, the presentation of the trial as global theatre also determined what was offered to readers in different countries.

Translation and the news

Although we may use the word 'translation' when referring to news translation, it is clear that what happens during the process of transfer is not
translation as generally understood. This helps to explain why journalists
object to being labelled as translators, and prefer to refer to anyone who
works across languages as an international journalist. The process of bringing
information out of one cultural context into another may involve an element
of interlingual transfer, but the focus is not on linguistic transferral; rather it
is on the transposition of information in a format aimed at meeting the
demands of the target readership. All kinds of additional textual processes
beyond the interlingual are involved, regardless of whether there is an
existing original text or whether the journalist is compiling a report from a
variety of sources.

The fact that there may not even be an original calls the very idea of
translation into question. If translating involves the transfer of a text produced in one language into another, then frequently what happens in news
reporting cannot be defined as translation in this way. Yet arguably there is a
translation dimension when a story that begins in one context is told, then
retold for other readers in another language somewhere else.

Even when there is a source text, the picture remains clouded. As we can
see from the examples given in this chapter of supposedly accurate translations taken from an original, the variations are so great as a result of various
textual manipulations that we have only a loose grasp of what that original
might have been.

What happens in news translation is that networks of foreign correspondents, working within or linked to news agencies, write and shape stories for
designated audiences. This mainly results in the creation of completely new
texts, which resist the definition of translation. The domination of certain
languages globally also means that power inequalities that exist in the socio-
political arena manifest themselves in textual strategies employed by international journalists. What the study of global news translation does, therefore,
is to make us all more aware of the manipulative processes that underlie
what we read and to raise serious questions about the extent to which we can
ever know what was or what was not said in another cultural context.

Appendix
The languages of global news

On 23 April 2004, an international symposium that aimed to explore the role of globalization, linguistic difference and translation in the production of news was held at the University of Warwick. This symposium was the first of a projected series that will explore aspects of the complex role of translation in global news communication. The symposia represent the public face of an AHRC-funded research project that will investigate the cultural politics and economics of language and translation in global media over a three-year period. Invited panellists were Professor Michael Cronin of Dublin City University, Professor Yves Gambier of Turku University, Finland, Mario Lubetkin, Director General of the Inter Press Service, Dr Daya Thussu of Goldsmiths College, London, Anthony Williams, Editor of Treasury News, Reuters, Eric Wishart, Editor-in-Chief of the Agence France-Presse, and Anne Wallace, a distinguished translator of financial and business news. A primary objective of the event was to bring together in dialogue academics and practitioners, journalists and translators, so as to explore different facets of the processes of international communication.

This report includes extracts from the taped presentations, together with highlights of the ensuing debate. Following the symposium, participants were invited to send further thoughts on both the event and the future direction of the research, and a sample of the responses is provided.

In the opening session, Eric Wishart and Anthony Williams provided some useful, concrete information on the organization of Agence France-Presse and Reuters, two of the three main international news agencies, the third being Associated Press. The role of news agencies in news gathering was highlighted from the outset: newspapers, radio and television cannot have journalists placed in every country of the world, hence the important role of news agencies which do, and so are primary sources of news gathering. AFP has about 160 bureaus worldwide and works in six languages: French, English, Spanish and Arabic, with some services in German and Portuguese.

Eric Wishart pointed out that AFP serves both as a domestic news agency in France and as an international agency. Having become independent in 1957, it has grown steadily and in 2003 for the first time received a higher percentage of income from international media than from French media, which he feels indicates a big shift that reflects the growing influence of English internationally. The AFP English service started in the late 1970s early 1980s, though the agency had always worked exclusively in English in Asia. In those early years, it was a translation-based service, and Wishart shared a story about his early experiences back in 1984:

> I was given news stories in French and asked to write English versions of them. Not word-by-word translations, which for someone who knows translation would mean a bad translation. Basically, we'd take the French story as rough notes and we'd write an English version. In the English service obviously we didn't have the same network as the French journalists did, and there were far more French journalists than there were English journalists, so we had to translate pretty quickly. The French felt it was a good idea that the English service consisted of translation from French, but pretty soon we saw that it really was not satisfactory. The journalists who did it had language skills but were not professional translators. Quite often the stories looked like bad translations. We also occasionally had translation errors – there was once an example when Joan of Arc [La Pucelle] came out as a little flea instead of the Maid of Orleans. We could see that if we wanted to beat Reuters, this was not the way to go, so for the last twenty years we've expanded the English service network and, as much as possible, we write it originally in English, which is more immediate, faster and better.

Wishart explained the stages of the news-gathering procedure, using as an example the divergent accounts of a serious train accident in North Korea which had just begun to appear in the world press on 22 April. The news came originally from the Chinese News Agency, in both Mandarin and English, and a figure of 3,000 casualties was given. Then AFP offices in China and South Korea started to receive reports and to translate them:

> So you've already got two steps: you've got the original story in Korean from the Korean News Agency, translated in the bureau by a Korean journalist who speaks English. The story is then translated again in the central editing desk in Hong Kong by a French writer, because there was no French writer in the Seoul bureau … And it's big news, Reuters are on the case, AP are on the case, so you've got to get the news out fast.

The speed and diversity of sources means that it is often difficult to check facts, and in the North Korean train crash incident, the final casualty figures were well below 100. Ensuring reliability of information is complicated by the need to get news out as fast as possible and by the shifts between languages. Translation is a crucial part of the transmission process:

In Japan, the big Japanese news agency which uses AFP buys the English service and then translates it into Japanese and redistributes it to Japanese clients ... All our new subscribers tend to work in English, but if the English-language service is not of a standard to compete with Reuters, we'll lose our clients altogether. They'll all go to AP or to Reuters ... We can't get away from translation in news agencies.

In Iraq, for example, AFP have used American journalists embedded with the US forces and Iraqi journalists inside Feluja who report in Arabic, phone through to the Baghdad AFP bureau where a bilingual Arab journalist takes the information in Arabic and then writes it in English, from which it is then translated into other languages.

At the same time, Wishart points out that all the reports have to be collated and turned into a homogeneous story:

I think on the general AFP newswire we probably run every day about 350,000 words – we count words more than stories – so if you multiply that by six services plus different targeted wires we have millions of words moving around the world every day in a constant state of translation ... We can say that we are multilingual, multicultural – we're a melting pot, so certainly not the voice of France. An Arabic writer reporting from Feluja is not going to work the same way as an American. The translation aspect really shows up quite important cultural differences in the treatment of news.

Those cultural differences can be seen in terms of stylistic difference. Wishart drew attention to the French practice of writing a story so as 'to keep the best bit to the last'. Where English readers expect to be given a statement at the start of a news item, which will then be expanded upon as the story is developed, the French expectation is for the denouement of the story to be retained until the end. Wishart gave as an example a hypothetical French news item about a president getting into his car, the car driving off in heavy rain and then, when an atmosphere of suspense has been created, in the final paragraph the president is shot dead by a waiting gunman. In the English version, the shooting would happen in the first paragraph and the story would then build on that knowledge. Translating clearly involves awareness of audience expectations and writerly conventions.

Anthony Williams began with intercultural jokes:

No conference on translation would be complete without a brief nod to the pleasures provided by mistranslation or at least misguided use of translation. Speakers of German will know why the drink Irish Mist did not sell well in German-speaking countries and Spanish speakers will understand why the Pajero jeep did not go down well in Latin America. There was also the advertisement for Parker pens – 'It won't leak in your pocket and embarrass you', which rendered into Spanish conveyed the reassuring message that it would not make you pregnant. My own favourite from personal experience was when I was covering the visit of a South African delegation to Switzerland in the 1980s. P. W. Botha was the Prime Minister and he was travelling with his Foreign Minister, Pik Botha. At a fairly hostile press conference, the PM was asked why the Pretoria government forced people to live in townships. P. W. looked perturbed and then answered, 'We don't force them to live there, we coerce them.' At which point Pik told him in a stage whisper, 'Convince them, Prime Minister, convince them.'

Williams pointed out that the translation of news is not a new phenomenon, and that the BBC, Radio Free Europe and Radio Liberty have been operating internationally for a long time, CNN has expanded its own offering of global news by linking up with local providers, while more recently Al-Jazeera has developed a news service for the Arab world in Arabic. Reuters works with a total of eighteen languages, though Williams drew attention to the fact that none of the 2,000-plus editorial staff is actually designated as a translator. The daily output is equivalent in volume terms to the Bible, and over 60 per cent of that material is in English, with Japanese coming second with 7 per cent.

If people providing news are not translators, what are they? The answer is journalists, editors or redacteurs. A typical Reuters bureau with a domestic language will be staffed by international staff writing about that country for an international audience and local-language reporters who report on similar issues for the local market. Their copy will then be complemented by local-language versions of stories from other date-lines, with the English-language copy used as a basis for that file. Clearly, translation in its most basic form is a requirement for this pro-cess. While the international correspondents need to be linguists to understand what is going on in the country where they are working, local staff need to be able to render the original English-language stories in German, French or whatever. But it is not translation pure and simple, rather the production of a news service, a news product in a specific language, tailored to a specific local audience and reflecting the journalistic norms in that region.

Like Wishart, Williams drew attention to stylistic factors and audience expectations. He pointed out that English readers like direct speech in quo-tation marks, whereas German readers prefer indirect speech. English read-ers like a densely information-packed opening paragraph, while German readers prefer succinct introductions, often in one short sentence.

No journalist of any experience would ever reproduce a press statement, but would always be aware of the need to rearrange and rewrite. Nevertheless, this practice can be problematic. Williams noted that novelists usually have some control over a translation of their work, whereas in the news business there is rarely ever time for such control:

> Fortunately, the style of agency journalism lends itself to this process, mainly by its tendency to use simple structures: who? where? what? why? when? and by its essential purpose of accurate, unbiased facts. Agency journalism is not polemical, and is aimed primarily at relating the facts as we know them without unnecessary embellishment.

Williams warned against machine translation, and word-for-word translation, though acknowledged that computers could be used for such texts as the CPI Index or Group Net profit. He also discussed cultural issues – false friends, where a word in one language seems to mean something similar in another, but actually means something quite different, translation of colloquialisms and the weight attached to informal language (both George Bush and Vladimir Putin use quite earthy language that causes problems for translators) and the sheer complexity involved in transferring news across several languages, where each transfer brings subtle (or not so subtle) shifts of meaning.

The second session was begun by Mario Lubetkin, who stated the aims of IPS as being those of global inclusion,

> to disseminate our information to more persons than we do now, and to achieve that goal we should overcome both linguistic and cultural barriers, so that a citizen from India or Burkina Faso might receive the information in his/her own language and in the way he/she considers it most suitable. The core activity of IPS is the production of independent news and analysis of world events and global processes affecting the economic, social and political development of peoples and nations, especially in the South. In the 70s and 80s we were the only or one of very few news agencies that focussed on so-called Third World countries, paying particular attention to human rights, gender and environmental issues. Our major clients were based in the South, particularly Latin America.

Today, IPS focusses on development issues, civil society questions and the effects of globalization. An editorial priority is to 'give a voice to the voiceless', hence the agency seeks out the opinions of a wide range of people. IPS works mainly in English and Spanish, but news is also disseminated in seventeen languages. Unlike other news agencies, IPS concentrates on three different markets: media outlets, civil society and international, local and regional institutions and organizations:

> It is a matter of understanding how to go from the global to the local and then go back to global without affecting the feelings of people and, in this case, users of information.

Lubetkin told the story of how, at the Earth Summit in Brazil in 1992, IPS produced a printed conference daily publication called *TerraViva*, and has continued to produce similar publications for international events. However, at the IV World Social Forum in India in January 2004, less than half the printed texts were picked up by participants, which led the editors to rethink their policy. Once a number of the stories had been translated into Hindi, response increased and distribution went up to 60,000 copies daily:

> This experience confirmed that we must not only focus on what we write but also on the ways in which we reach our readers, so that both form and contents meet their expectations ... We will continue to advocate respect for cultural diversity in the field of news and communications.

In her presentation, Anne Wallace looked at the multifaceted role of the translator, and in particular at the responsibility that a translator carries. At one end of the scale, journalists in a local office will often be called upon to translate a key quote that will move the markets. She cited the case of a news item deriving from the London-based *Al-Quds* paper, in which Al-Qaeda claimed responsibility for the Istanbul bomb blast in the autumn of 2003, an announcement which had both a political and an economic impact. At the other end of the scale, translators work in partnership with news providers and can offer insights into what is happening in a particular country. Part of her job when working for Reuters was to select and translate stories that added local flavour and opinions. Such stories, in her view, could be seen as 'asides', but she gave a number of examples that showed how the decision of a translator to edit material can have enormous impact. Such work, she suggests, is 'more than a literal translation', for the translator has to research the material and both cut and add material in order to enhance understanding.

In the financial world, attitudes to translation vary. Investment banks want information translated, but they also want the contents to be literally translated into English so that the analysts' recommendations are represented in good faith. The translator is therefore called upon at times to be a journalist, editing and shaping material, at other times to be a good and faithful servant to the source:

> Translators play a huge variety of roles to ensure that global news is accessible to an international readership, from providing the key quote in a breaking story to adding local flavour for investors, from informing government bodies to giving a voice to the often ignored regions of the world and helping companies gain market share and increase market awareness.
>
> Two key issues for the success of in-house translation desks are who is footing the bill and what is the group's raison d'être. BBC Monitoring translators are paid by the BBC World Service, the FCO and the MOD, i.e. by the taxpayer, in order to provide a service to the government.

Private news groups have to make money to please their shareholders. Therefore, translated news must be able to generate income.

Wallace drew attention to the halving of Reuters' translation desk by 1996, from a staff of thirty-two to just sixteen. By the end of the 1990s, the trend was towards setting up a core service of local languages. IPS has maintained its translation service, in order to give a voice to the South.

Daya Thussu talked about language in global television news. In a richly illustrated presentation he showed how translation in television news is not just about language but also about the transfer of ideas, values and a worldview. He began by introducing briefly a discussion about the commercial values that underpinned Rupert Murdoch's Star Television news channel in India and his manipulation of the complex language situation in the country, which has eighteen official languages, to create a mass market for television:

> When Murdoch's media entered the Indian market in early 1990, India was opening up its broadcasting environment in one of the world's most controlled broadcasting systems. Although it was and is a functioning democracy, the airwaves were totally controlled by the State. They began with standard BBC World News. And nobody was interested in it apart from 0.5 per cent of English speakers. So then they started to Indianize. Murdoch realized that if he had to go beyond the kind of Delhi–Bombay metropolitan to reach the masses he would actually have to go native. And that's exactly what they did. And it's very interesting how native they did go. I mean how quickly they did it is really amazing. You had a very ruthless, aggressive media mogul who was not particularly bothered about local culture in the sense that he had a global agenda. India was part of the bigger plan, getting into Asian markets. But he was not interested in the subtlety of India's language system. He was interested in money. So he goes for the top language, which is Hindi.

Murdoch started with a news service provided by a network called MDTV, one of the best television networks in India. It had a dedicated twenty-four-hour news channel in English and Hindi. When Murdoch realized that only a tiny minority of the working middle class of India and the diaspora would watch Star News to find out what was happening back home, he went for indigenization. Thussu showed a short clip of a promotional ad for Star News in Hindi. The Bollywood-style song, roughly translated, says: 'We keep you in the forefront, we go behind the news. The audience is at the heart of this.' The culturally familiar style of the ad made Star News the most popular television news network in India.

Thussu criticized the channel for undermining the public-service values of the national state broadcaster:

The issue is they might be doing it in their own language, but the kind of values that they are promoting are actually based on a certain type of legitimization of certain types of values, which is free market. And they're very, very clear about that. The government is bad, business is good. Private is good. Public is bad. They're saying this in Hindi. They're saying it in Bollywood style.

This description led into a discussion about conceptual translation, or the translation of ideas or values. Thussu commented on the CNN phenomenon that has been copied around the world by other news networks such as ITV, Sky, Euronews, Al-Jazeera, Al Arabiya and Star:

We're living in this kind of 24/7 news environment and because of the power of the visuals they are reaching really global audiences. But where do they get their footage? Television is an expensive business. More than 80 per cent of what you see on screens around the world comes from two news agencies: Reuters TV and Associated Press Television News.

In addition to the advent of twenty-four-hour news there have been some fundamental changes since news networks have been taken over by media conglomerates. Thussu argued the concentration of media ownership becomes complicated when geo-strategic interests are involved, particularly at a time when alternative ideas are not making a huge difference. He showed a clip from Al-Jazeera's transmission of Tony Blair's speech soon after the Americans started bombing Afghanistan in 2001. The speech was broadcast with simultaneous interpretation into Arabic:

So that's [24/7] news for you and it's going live. When the President of the US is talking to his countrymen he's talking to people in Africa, he's talking to people in India, he's talking to people in Asia. And it's being translated, as you saw in the case of Al-Jazeera, it's translated instantly into local languages.

To demonstrate his point that the conceptual translation of global news is a structural one, Thussu played two very similar clips of a story transmitted by CNN and Star TV in India:

The point is footage is being provided by the same people, the Pentagon provides footage, 'look we're going to bomb this country' and this is the footage they give to major news agencies and they then send it around the world. So when we talk about global news flow and barriers to that, I think the biggest barrier is the existing structure. How it's structured, which defines how the world is shaped, and mass media, particularly television, is absolutely central to that.

Reflecting on some of the issues raised by his colleagues, Michael Cronin shifted attention back to the changing nature of translation in today's world. Noting that languages rise and decline in status, he questioned whether this trend contradicts the equation between language, culture and place that has been traditionally held. This is taken from his symposium:

> If one of the historical duties of translation has been to translate a particular culture that is linked to a particular place, how do we square that with this other historical function, the ability of translation to universalize, its ability to take things out of a particular culture at a specific time and in a specific place? A point made over and over today is that translation makes people aware of the nature and depth of individual cultures in two ways: translating out of a culture, you show its riches, translating inwards you bring in things that can reveal hidden potential in that culture. So translation is caught between the particularizing drive of translating into something that is culturally appropriate and the universalizing drive that makes the richness of a culture available to others. It's a sort of pentecostal moment, when someone's on the top floor of a building, they rush down and lo and behold, they can preach in any number of languages, so that at this moment of conversion, universalization becomes possible.

Cronin suggested that two key issues emerging from the symposium were, on the one hand, the risk of translation becoming merely instrumental, given the constraints of time and the need to have news in circulation as fast as possible and, on the other hand, the risk of forgetting what he terms 'the universalizing mission that goes beyond cultures and places and times'.

A fundamental issue that came out in all the discussions concerned the definition of translation. There were clear differences between speakers and participants over this issue. Williams explained that Reuters rarely uses what he terms 'pure professional translators', while Wishart declared that where there are translators in AFP, 'they are usually imposed by the state'. Referring back to the Korean train incident, he pointed out that in countries such as China or North Korea there is a reticence to speak to foreigners. Hence the role of interpreters and translators has assumed more importance than in other, less centrally controlled societies. Williams argued that there was a great need for language journalists rather than translators. Citing the case of recordings supposedly made by Osama Bin Laden, he described the special skills needed to understand the connotations of such a text:

> With Bin Laden we have a lot of difficulty making sense of what is said in that kind of Koranic Arabic. We got the major lines, but there was an Arabic-speaking journalist with knowledge of the Koran who picked up the references. You had to listen to it two or three times to really get what Bin Laden was trying to say. So it's not just pure translation. You

need a cultural background. You need somebody who can read the Koranic references, somebody with news sense. With a professional translator who wasn't a journalist it would be a very laborious procedure ... If you get 100,000 words in some language, you don't want 100,000 or 150,000 words in English. You need someone who can understand it and give you the main points very fast.

Cronin noted that this transformed translation into a virtual process, rather than one of mediation. Anne Wallace and Anthony Williams both took up Wishart's point, and drew attention to the term 'translator-abstractor' as used by Reuters. The primary task of such a role is to sift through the material produced in a given language, to find the principal story or stories, the nugget as it is termed, and then to represent that material for English readers in such a way that key points are highlighted.

There was some discussion of the use of photographs to illustrate news items and variations in journalistic practice. Then the questioning shifted back to mistranslation. Cronin made the valuable point that mistranslation is one of the ways in which translation becomes visible, since otherwise 'its very success makes it invisible'. Wishart gave an example of the mistranslation of the word 'casualty', which was taken to mean 'fatality' in one story. Questions were raised as to whether the demand for twenty-four-hour breaking news had an impact on the quality of translation, but this was rebutted by the news agency representatives, who said that speed and news delivery had always been an equation. Rather than a decline in quality, what has happened is that there are more stringent rules and the checking of sources.

Yves Gambier led a session that focussed more on ethical issues and on the vexed question of independence. He and Mario Lubetkin discussed the question of what is meant by global news and how stories and illustrations are selected. Lubetkin pointed out that many local news agencies around the world had disappeared. Hence the task of representing small countries and regional and local stories is more difficult. IPS has chosen to concentrate on producing items that are more discursive rather than short news items:

> Our stories are not short. They are long, 1,000 words each story, but they are features, with all the elements, what's happened after the media has received a story from, say, Reuters. We complement the information received by the big news agencies, by what the West writes. We are not big, but the point is that we want to play a role in the big picture.

The discussion was animated and could have gone on much longer than the space allowed in a single day. Participants were invited to send in their thoughts on the event, along with suggestions for future development, and the very thoughtful responses received are included below.

Reflections on the day

I found the symposium very interesting and I believe vital questions have been raised. Personally, I was surprised by the attitude towards translation that large press agencies have. Local correspondents write their press releases directly in English, which usually is not their native language, other journalists then *adapt* the story they get from the central agency. Then a press release usually undergoes two translations/adaptations not carried out by trained translators. For sure, important press agencies choose not to employ translators not because they lack money or do not know a good translation will be carried out by a professional translator. Their reason is that their clients want *adapted* press releases. And that can only account for a public who likes to read or listen to adapted versions of what is going on, versions that do not require effort to understand other cultures, versions endlessly reconfirming the same values.

It was very interesting to see that Inter Press Service, less interested in giving out the breaking news as quickly as possible and aiming at the high quality of the information provided, shows more interest in translation. By this I do not mean to say that other agencies' work is of lower quality, only their main goal is to be quick, which implies being less precise and having to rectify more often. Inter Press Service seems to allow more time in order to get precise information, which requires translation.

I am convinced that the issues raised during the symposium go far beyond the field of translation studies. Still, translation seems to be the core of it all, paradoxically because in a sense it is absent from the process. The practice of translation often requires the intervention of translators who are skilled in other fields, web localization is one example. But, if I believe it is good to choose translators who are experts in adapting the text for marketing purposes, I do not believe adapting news can be considered good practice as, in my opinion, adapted news can no longer be objective, unless news is considered a commodity, requiring marketing techniques in order to be sold better. The first temporary conclusion I personally have drawn from the symposium is that the absence of translators as such from the main press agencies proves that news does not really need to remain as similar and as objective as possible, but, on the contrary, mainly needs to be sold. If clients want adapted versions of events, journalists who know a foreign language will tailor the news item to their needs.

Nevertheless, I have hopes for the future thanks to the fact that representatives of press agencies during the symposium have expressed interest in translation and the fact that more and more people know foreign languages and can easily access the foreign press through the internet, which might create a readership more interested in news that is translated rather than adapted.

(M. Cristina Caimotto)

The symposium provided an insight into two aspects of language and global news: on the one hand, the overall ideological, political and indeed ethical issues that arise from the very concept of global news and their representation and transmission, on the other hand, the workface concerns of 'accuracy' and temporal constraints that underpin the work of news producers, journalists and language professionals (I am deliberately avoiding the use of the term 'translator' here in view of what follows). Such concerns were made very clear by the representatives of news agencies. These two perspectives made for a very interesting and stimulating symposium.

On a more negative note, however (and I tend to think that my concerns here are shared by 'academic' colleagues involved in researching translation and training translators and interpreters), I was disappointed to see how different the metalanguage of the 'practitioners' and users of news translations was from that of translation researchers (who, in many cases, happen to be practitioners themselves). To put it bluntly, we did not mean the same thing by 'translation'. Or, in other words, translation for the 'workface' seemed to end where it would have started for me! Almost as if translation for the users (and the translator herself!) were associated with the puzzling concept of 'pure translation' (nothing to do with Benjamin here!), or more worryingly literal translation. When translation became context-sensitive, culturally aware, a real attempt at communication (what we teach our students to do, what we think the object of our study is), it seems that it had to be renamed, called something else, lose its 'negative' connotations (a phenomenon that has been associated with the increasing use of the term 'localization'). The same applied to the 'translator' herself who was then granted the title of 'translator/editor', or 'translator/abstractor'(?) as soon as her work entailed more than linguistic correspondence.

And finally, it was clear from the various talks and the discussions they generated that the concept itself of the 'translator' was unclear. The translator was in some cases the individual whose work might or might not be edited, but in other cases her work was part and parcel of that of the journalist, or the editorial team. The translations were performed by qualified translators, professional linguists, journalists, etc.

PS: I remember hearing that one of the problems, for instance in the case of Arabic-language news, was dialect variations. Although this might indeed be a problem in terms of oral language, the language of the press (be it written or broadcast) is standard Arabic, whatever the country. There are indeed some regional variations in the choice of terms but these would be of the same scale as, say, variations that exist within the Francophone press. I had to leave before the end of the symposium and did not manage to make the point!

(Dr Miriam Salama-Carr, University of Salford, UK)

The main purpose of this symposium was to explore the role of globalization, linguistic difference and translation in the production of news. The first speakers (Wishart, Williams and Wallace) offered us an interesting view on the work of the translation process in practice. How does a news agency work? What is the main role of a translator in the newsmaking process? What difficulties do they encounter? Not every participant at this meeting (the public varied from students to teachers, from translators to communication scholars, from researchers and theoreticians to people with practical experience and/or a combination of all these) was aware of the complex processes that transform an event into a global news message. One of the most interesting questions was whether and how a translator 'can tell the story as it is' and how his/her duty is prescribed, compared to traditional journalists. Despite the fact that the speakers were not unanimous, this question made us think about the overall role of the translator and the main objects in the global newsmaking process. It was a good choice to start with these speakers, even if sometimes the anecdotes were a bit too present in the stories of the journalists. All questions that tended to generalize and structure the anecdotes were answered with an anecdote.

That need was partly covered by the most interesting presentations of the day, by Michael Cronin and Daya Thussu, who both presented a framework that enlarged the role and function of news and translation, i.e. that enlarged our view on these phenomena, especially on the social and political consequences. Both presentations made clear that a strong academic input is necessary to complement stories from practical experience.

For a follow-up, we would suggest focussing on two points:

1. research on common grounds between translation studies and communication studies (i.e. the socio-political topic as mentioned above)
2. the role the traditional journalist and translator still can play within this new digital reality of the internet and global news flows.

(Luc van Doorslaer, Michaël Opgenhaffen at
Lessius Hogeschool, Belgium)

At the recent symposium hosted by the Centre for Translation and Comparative Cultural Studies to explore the role of globalization and translation in the production of international news, a number of issues were raised inviting further academic discussion. The event also suggested some other potential avenues worthy of additional exploration.

The panel of insiders airing views on the translation of news rightly placed emphasis on the importance of journalistic skills in the presentation of news, most often the know-how and experience of the journalist rather than the linguist/translator. Less attention was perhaps given to the subject of change of meaning that often accompanies a message when crossing cultural and political boundaries. In the case of English, news items relating to the war in Iraq have been known to have been reported differently in the British and the American news media. Whereas this divergence in intra-lingual translation may be the result of cultural and political factors, interlingual conveyance of news is in addition often influenced on a more subtle, exclusively linguistic level. As research has shown in studies of court interpretation, incomplete sentences, pauses and hesitation are often left unaccounted for by interpreters, unaware that in delivering a 'tidied up' account of a defendant's statement, translated records do not always truly represent the nature of the original. The same situation is likely to apply to the conveyance of information in written form. Translators from other languages into English, even closely related European languages, also need to heed the favoured understated mode of British English which may easily misread a speaker's neutral request as impolite, the translation having failed to provide sufficient indirect embedding, e.g. 'I don't mind' is not infrequently intended to mean 'I'd like to'.

In the afternoon's discussion concerned with globalization, communication and international news, the importance of another factor was aptly illustrated. The recent worldwide development in the electronic media has now established English as the global language and, in particular following the recent European enlargement, the lingua franca of Europe. As was effectively illustrated at the symposium, two options are now available: the language of McDonald's and the values accompanying it, versus the use of a national language.

Whenever there are options inherent in the transfer of news between languages, there is also the opportunity of political appropriation, as is already well documented in audio-visual translation and the factors that have sometimes determined the choice of dubbing in preference to subtitling as a political means to withhold the true nature of the original message. So also in the field of interpreting. On 23 May this year, reporting on a visit to a Stockholm mosque, one of the leading Swedish daily papers carried the heading: 'Double messages in the mosque'. While in Arabic the speaker referred to 'the rape of Islam by the United States', in the interpreter's Swedish rendition this became 'the repudiation of the US torture of political prisoners'.

In written as well as spoken messages, language in itself only has the power that we choose to invest in it.

(Gunilla Anderman, Professor of Translation Studies, University of Surrey)

Translation in global news and languages of global news

The symposium looked at two themes – translation in global news and languages of global news. Most of the day was spent debating translation in global news while one session looked at how media mogul Rupert Murdoch decided to 'go native' and broadcast in Hindi to gain a strong presence in India.

Types of media

The symposium concentrated on news agency and television output. There was a notable juxtaposition in that news agencies' raison d'être is to provide stories to other professional news providers, whilst television targets the general public. This raised interesting issues about use of language and its motivation.

Translation integral to providing global news

The clearest message from the symposium is that translation is integral to providing global news, a good example being the North Korean train blast on 22 April 2004. The story was broken in Korean and then sent to the news agencies' local bureaus based in Hong Kong (AFP) or Singapore (Reuters) where the story was translated and written in English and French and then sent out on the wire to be used and translated by media around the globe.

Journalists recoil at the thought of being a translator

Journalists do not see themselves as translators at all and in fact the term translator/translation is viewed as a bad word, according to Eric Wishart, editor-in-chief of AFP. Translation is merely a tool in a journalist's armoury of which more important tools are an excellent news sense and good writing skills.

Poor perception of translators

Translators are often held in low regard – either perceived as writing bad copy or told by state-controlled governments (such as in China or Burma) to act as informers. Translators wishing to work in global news should also train to be journalists. The Inter Press Service (IPS), which currently uses translators, is looking to change the way their translators work so that they have a better news sense.

Journalists view translation very differently to academics

There is a large gulf between the way that those on the job and academics view translation. News agencies are very keen to take on language graduates who they then train to be journalists. Newsagency journalists use their language skills to assemble the necessary elements to write their news stories but it is not given much conscious thought (except when there has been a bad or a mistranslation). There has been little or no interaction between academics and news providers. The project examining translation in global news is, therefore, breaking new ground as it has started a debate about why and how news is translated and its impact on global perceptions.

(Anne Wallace, translator)

Report placed on AHRC project website: http://www2.warwick.ac.uk/fac/arts/ctccs/research/tgn/events/2004/

Notes

2 Globalization and translation

1 Scholte also points out that supraterritorial connectivity does not imply that territorial space is no longer important, indicating that at present global relations substantially rather than wholly transcend territorial space and pointing to parallel processes of reterritorialization, like for example urbanization and the growth of globally connected cities (2005: 75–77).

2 Giddens asserts, in this respect: 'Time was still connected with space (and place) until the uniformity of time measurement by the mechanical clock was matched by uniformity in the social organisation of time. This shift coincided with the expansion of modernity and was not completed until the current century' (1991a: 17–18).

3 In this respect, it would be interesting to investigate more closely how the main means for the transmission of written information in modernity, print and electronic transmission, shape specific forms of disembedded social relations.

4 Cf. K. Marx, *Capital*, Vol. 2. The circulation sphere is effectively the marketplace, where commodities are transformed into money and vice versa. While value, according to Marx, can only be generated in the sphere of production through human labour, in the circulation sphere a social relation between the producers appears as a social relation between things and commodities seem endowed with a life of their own. Marx has analysed this in terms of commodity fetishism (1976, *Capital*, Vol. 1, pp. 163–77).

5 In dealing with recent developments in telecommunications, Held et al. remark:

> none of this telecommunications infrastructure could really facilitate regularized global communications if it were not accompanied by a further form of collective infrastructure – shared languages and linguistic competencies ... it is the existence of shared languages or language capacities that is the key infrastructure of intercultural communication and interaction.
>
> (1999: 345)

6 31.2 per cent of internet users in the world are English speakers. They are followed at a considerable distance by Chinese speakers (15.7 per cent), Spanish speakers (8.7 per cent) and Japanese speakers (7.4 per cent). However, use by non-English speakers, especially Chinese, Spanish, French, Portuguese and Arabic, is experiencing a much higher growth than use by English speakers (Source: Internet World Stats, www.internetworldstats.com, figures updated June 2007). Estimates indicate that over half of all internet content is in English, although figures can only be arrived at indirectly: a Funredes study of 2000 based on results obtained from searching a sample of words in different languages in the major search engines estimates total internet English content in 52 per cent (www.funredes.org).

7 Similar perspectives on the articulation of the global and the local in related areas of cultural theory can be found in Homi Bhabha's discussion of mimicry as erosion of the master's language in colonial discourse (1994), Néstor García Canclini's study of the changing meaning of crafts in Mexico from products for self-consumption within indigenous communities to commodities that are sold to tourists (1982) and James Clifford's approach to museums as contact zones and his discussion of how this Western institution is adapted to local cultural traditions across the world (1997).

3 Globalization and news: the role of the news agencies in historical perspective

1 Paul-Louis Bret, founder and head of the independent Agence France-Afrique in 1941 and briefly of AFP in 1947, maintained the importance of an independent agency founded on the right to information, related to a notion of objectivity understood as reporting without commentary or interpretation. The idea of news provision as a public service, which should accordingly be supplied independently of economic gain, is also put forward by Donald Read in his account of the history of Reuters (1999) and by Ignacio Muro Benayas in his recent book on news agencies, which is subtitled 'Between Business and General Interest' (2006).
2 The narration of the murder of the Kinck family in 1869, and of the subsequent investigation, trial and execution of the man found guilty of their murder, Troppmann, inaugurated the mass success of the crime *fait-divers* (Palmer, 1983: 29–32).
3 The telegraph was indispensable not only for ever-increasing business communications and news, but also became a valuable tool of diplomacy. For an account of how the telegraph changed diplomacy see Nickles (2003).
4 In these early alliances we find the historical roots of the prominent presence of global agencies in certain territories beyond their old imperial dominions, such as for example Agence France-Presse in South America.
5 As Michael Schudson (1978) argues in his penetrating study of the history of American newspapers, the ideal of objectivity has significantly changed over time, being first used after the First World War to question journalism's naive belief in the neutrality of facts and information and highlighting the importance of interpretation and method, and coming under attack in the 1960s, when it was shown that objective reporting was built on hidden assumptions and served to reinforce official viewpoints of social reality.
6 Palmer (1998) has excellently documented this in a chapter on the role of Havas and Reuters in Russia at the beginning of the twentieth century.
7 The history of both France-Presse and Reuters has been characterized by long periods during which the price of subscriptions has been frozen. Read even states that, in these conditions in which subscriptions are kept much lower than costs, Reuters provides an indirect public service to and through the press (1999: 309). This is of course explicitly recognized in the case of AFP, which receives about half of its total income from the French government.
8 Ian Macdowell, former chief news editor of Reuters, responded pragmatically to the question of whether Reuters was a Western-looking organization, rather than a world agency, posed in relation to its coverage of the events in Tiananmen Square in 1989 by stating: 'If we cater primarily for the West it should not be because of ethnic or cultural bias but because we pay most attention to the needs of those clients who pay us most for our services' (quoted in Read, 1999: 470).
9 For a history of the channel, see Miles (2005).

4 Translation in global news agencies

1 For example, Donald Read's history of Reuters emphasizes the multilingual skills of figures like George Douglas Williams, who joined the editorial staff in 1861

with a fluent command of French, Italian and Spanish, and who was sent to Florence, then transferred to Paris, to become chief editor in 1875; Henry Collins, who joined in 1862 'after polishing up his French and German', although he mostly worked within the English-speaking British Empire, becoming general manager for India before being appointed general manager for Australia; Walter F. Bradshaw, who joined Reuters in 1874 with a good command of Spanish and Portuguese, was sent to Chile to help establish the South American service (Read, 1999: 32–33).

2 Reuters has other media products such as online reports in Arabic, Chinese, English, French, German, Italian, Japanese, Korean, Portuguese, Russian and Spanish.

3 Conveniently, as André Lefevere points out, 'the term rewriting absolves us of the necessity to draw borderlines between various forms of rewriting, such as "translation", "adaptation", "emulation"' (1992: 47).

4 This is why the dateline, which certifies that the journalist is where the facts took place, that he or she is a witness of the events, has a key importance in agency journalism.

5 This figure is an extreme case and a good illustration of Daniel Simeoni's assertion that 'the translator has become the quintessential servant: efficient, punctual, hardworking, silent and yes, invisible' (1998: 12).

6 Another instance in which translation delays or hinders global news flow leading to confusion and the dissemination of inaccurate, or plainly erroneous information is that of mistranslation. News agencies have to be especially vigilant, because any errors they might make will be reproduced by subscribing organizations. An example can be found in EFE's mistranslation of Donald Rumsfeld's declaration concerning the risk of a terrorist attack in the US in the summer 2004. Rumsfeld alluded to the attacks in Spain to refer to the possibility of the US being attacked, which was translated as a warning of possible new attacks in Spain (*El Mundo*, 10/06/2004). In the case of the diffusion of inaccurate information (and this includes mistranslation) news agencies are obliged to circulate an immediate withdrawal (a 'kill', if the story is totally wrong) or correction to their clients as soon as the error is detected.

7 Neither of these terms is normally used in journalistic contexts, where the view of the journalist as news editor (which comprises the task of translation) prevails.

8 The relationship between (literary) writing and translating, involving the interchange not just of learning and creativity but also of prestige and recognition in complex ways in what are essentially inseparable activities has been recently explored by Susan Bassnett (2006), who views translation as part of the continuum of a writer's life. No similar accounts exist as yet on the relationship between journalistic or – equally important – academic writing and translating.

9 This is a form of internationalization, defined as the process of generalizing a product so that it can handle multiple languages and cultural conventions without the need for redesign (Pym, 2004: 29).

10 Manuals consulted are the following: *A Handbook of Reuters Journalism, AFP Manual del Servicio Español, IPS Style Manual*, access to which was generously provided by journalists of these organizations. They are respectively referred to in the references in the text as Reuters, AFP and IPS.

11 This is probably related to the fact that, in the case of AFP, the consulted manual is the one used by its Spanish desk, which is responsible for the translation of news from the English and French wires into Spanish. In the case of Reuters, the manual corresponds to the English-language service.

12 The only general reference to how translations should be done in AFP's *Manual* is the following: 'Debe tenerse especial cuidado en evitar los galicismos y los anglicismos en las traducciones y, en la medida de lo posible, no utilizar localismos

incomprensibles en otros países de lengua española si existen términos comprensibles en toda la región. Se recomienda el uso del diccionario a fin de verificar si tal o cual expresión existe en castellano o si se trata de un localismo que sólo se entiende en una región' (p. 73) ('One must be especially careful to avoid Gallicisms and Anglicisms in translations and, wherever possible, not to use localisms that would not be understood in other Spanish-speaking countries if terms exist that can be understood in the whole region. The use of a dictionary in order to verify whether an expression exists in Spanish or is rather a localism that can only be understood in one region is recommended.'). Reuters' *Handbook* does not contain any indication of this kind.

5 Journalism and translation: practices, strategies and values in the news agencies

1 Although in recent years the internet has been changing the nature of its public, and the presence of European readers has sharply increased. In particular, the Madrid attacks of 11 March 2004 generated a new readership from Spain.
2 This refers only to information not specifically related to Latin America in the first place, which is already rendered in Spanish by the two Spanish-language correspondents AFP has in its Washington office.

6 Reading translated news: an analysis of agency texts

1 News agencies classify items of breaking news according to their priority: a bulletin or alert is the highest priority item; an urgent or newsbreak is a priority two item or a contextualization of a previous alert; an update or lead (although lead also designates in agency journalism the opening paragraph of a story) writes through earlier reports by adding new information and/or context.
2 In this study, the first text, in which the translator's name appears second, has been classified as a translation, while the first, in which the translator's name appears first and which is a substantially different account according to the perception of someone who was also present, has been classified as an original text.

Bibliography

AFP. (2000). *Manual del Servicio Español*. Montevideo.

Alvarez, R. and Vidal, M. C. A. (eds). (1996). *Translation, Power, Subversion*. Clevedon: Multilingual Matters.

Anderson, B. (1983). *Imagined Communities*. London: Verso.

Appadurai, A. (1996). *Modernity at Large: Cultural Dimensions of Globalization*. Minneapolis and London: University of Minnesota Press.

Apter, E. (2001a). Balkan Babel: Translation Zones, Military Zones. *Public Culture*, 13(1), 65–80.

——(2001b). On Translation in a Global Market. *Public Culture*, 13(1), 1–12.

——(2006). *The Translation Zone*. Princeton and Oxford: Princeton University Press.

Baker, M. (1996). Linguistics and Cultural Studies: Complementary or Competing Paradigms in Translation Studies. In A. Lauer, H. Gerzymisch-Arbogast, J. Haller and E. Steiner (eds), *Übersetzungswissenschaft im Umbruch: Festschrift für Wolfram Wilss*. Tübingen: Gunter Narr.

——(2006). *Translation and Conflict: A Narrative Account*. London and New York: Routledge.

Bassnett, S. (2002). *Translation Studies* (third edition). London: Routledge.

——(2004). Trusting Reporters: What Exactly Did Saddam Say? *The Linguist*, 43(6), 176–78.

——(2005a). Bringing the News Back Home: Strategies of Acculturation and Foreignisation. *Language and Intercultural Communication*, 5(2), 120–30.

——(2005b). Translating Terror. *Third World Quarterly*, 26(3), 393–403.

——(2006). Writing and Translating. In S. Bassnett and P. Bush (eds), *The Translator as Writer* (pp. 173-83). London and New York: Continuum.

Bassnett, S. and Lefevere, A. (eds). (1990). *Translation, History and Culture*. New York: Pinter.

——(1998). *Constructing Cultures: Essays on Literary Translation*. Clevedon: Multilingual Matters.

Bauman, Z. (1989). *Legislators and Interpreters*. Cambridge: Polity Press.

——(1990). Modernity and Ambivalence. *Theory, Culture and Society*, 7, 143–69.

——(1998). *Globalization: The Human Consequences*. Cambridge: Polity Press.

Beck, U. (2000). *What is Globalization?* Cambridge: Polity.

Bhabha, H. K. (1994). *The Location of Culture*. London: Routledge.

Bielsa, E. (2005). Globalisation and Translation: A Theoretical Approach. *Language and Intercultural Communication*, 5(2), 131–44.

——(2006a). Global News Channels. In R. Robertson and J. A. Scholte (eds), *Encyclopedia of Globalization*. New York: Routledge.

——(2006b). Globalisation and News Translation: The Role of the News Agencies. *Norwich Papers*, 14, 15–28.

——(2007). Translation in Global News Agencies. *Target*, 19(1), 135–55.

Bourdieu, P. (1992). *Language and Symbolic Power*. Cambridge: Polity Press.

——(1993). *The Field of Cultural Production*. Cambridge: Polity Press.

——(1998). *On Television and Journalism*. London: Pluto.

——(2002). Les conditions sociales de la circulation internationale des idées. *Actes de la Recherche en Sciences Sociales*, 145, 3–8.

Bourdieu, P. and Wacquant, L. (2001). NewLiberalSpeak: Notes on the New Planetary Vulgate. *Radical Philosophy*, (105), 2–5.

Boyd-Barrett, O. (1980). *The International News Agencies*. London: Sage.

——(1997). Global News Wholesalers as Agents of Globalization. In A. Sreberny-Mohammadi, D. Winseck, J. McKenna and O. Boyd-Barrett (eds), *Media in Global Context: A Reader* (pp. 131–44). London: Arnold.

——(1998). 'Global' News Agencies. In O. Boyd-Barrett and T. Rantanen (eds), *The Globalization of News* (pp. 19–34). London: Sage.

Boyd-Barrett, O. and Rantanen, T. (eds). (1998). *The Globalization of News*. Londoni: Sage.

——(2004). News Agencies as News Sources: A Re-Evaluation. In C. Paterson and A. Sreberny (eds), *International News in the 21st Century* (pp. 31–45). Eastleigh: University of Luton Press.

Boyd-Barrett, O. and Thussu, D. K. (1992). *Contra-flow in Global News*. London: John Libbey.

Castells, M. (2000a). *The Information Age, Volume 1: The Rise of the Network Society* (second edition). Oxford: Blackwell.

Castells, M. (2000b). *The Information Age, Volume 2: Economy, Society and Culture, Vol. 1, The Rise of the Network Society* (second edition). Oxford: Blackwell.

Chalaby, J. K. (1996). Journalism as an Anglo-American Invention. *European Journal of Communication*, 11(3), 303–26.

——(ed.). (2005). *Transnational Television Worldwide*. London, New York: I. B. Tauris.

Cheyfitz, E. (1991). *The Poetics of Imperialism: Translation and Colonization from The Tempest to Tarzan*. New York and London: Oxford University Press.

Clausen, L. (2003). *Global News Production*. Copenhagen: Copenhagen Business School Press.

——(2004). Localizing the Global: 'Domestication' Processes in International News Production. *Media, Culture and Society*, 26(1), 25–44.

Clifford, J. (1997). *Routes: Travel and Translation in the Late Twentieth Century*. Cambridge, Mass.: Harvard University Press.

Crane, D., Kawashima, N. and Kawasaki, K. (2002). *Global Culture: Media, Arts, Policy and Globalization*. New York: Routledge.

Cronin, M. (2000). *Across the Lines: Travel, Language, Translation*. Cork: Cork University Press.

——(2003). *Translation and Globalization*. London and New York: Routledge.

——(2005). Burning the House Down: Translation in a Global Setting. *Language and Intercultural Communication*, 5(2), 108–19.

——(2006). *Translation and Identity*. London and New York: Routledge.

de la Motte, D. (1999). Utopia Commodified. In D. de la Motte and J. M. Przyblyski (eds), *Making the News: Modernity and the Mass Press in Nineteenth-Century France* (pp. 141–59). Amherst: University of Massachusetts Press.

Demers, D. (ed.). (2003). *Terrorism, Globalization and Mass Communication*. Spokane, Wash.: Marquette Books.

Even-Zohar, I. (1990). Polysystems Studies. *Poetics Today*, 11(1).

Featherstone, M. (ed.). (1990). *Global Culture: Nationalism, Globalization and Modernity*. London: Sage.

Friedman, J. (2002). Globalisation and the Making of a Global Imaginary. In G. Stald and T. Tufte (eds), *Global Encounters: Media and Cultural Transformation* (pp. 13–31). Luton: University of Luton Press.

Gambier, Y. (2006). 'Transformations in International News'. Paper presented at the Translation in Global News Conference, University of Warwick.

García Canclini, N. (1982). *Las culturas populares en el capitalismo*. Havana: Casa de las Américas.

García González, J. E. (2005). Palabra, espacio y tiempo. In C. Cortés Zaborras and M. J. Hernández Guerrero (eds), *La traducción periodística* (pp. 137–54). Cuenca: Ediciones de la Universidad de Castilla-La Mancha.

García Suárez, P. (2005). Noticias de agencia: algunos problemas planteados en la traducción español-árabe. In C. Cortés Zaborras and M. J. Hernández Guerrero (eds), *La traducción periodística* (pp. 175–97). Cuenca: Ediciones de la Universidad de Castilla-La Mancha.

Gentzler, E. (2001). *Contemporary Translation Theories* (revised second edition). Clevedon: Multilingual Matters.

Giddens, A. (1991a). *The Consequences of Modernity*. Cambridge: Polity.

——(1991b). *Modernity and Self-Identity*. Cambridge: Polity Press.

Giffard, C. A. (1998). Alternative News Agencies. In O. Boyd-Barrett and T. Rantanen (eds), *The Globalization of News* (pp. 191–201). London: Sage.

Giffard, C. A. and Nancy R. (2000). News Agencies, National Images, and Global Media Events. *Journalism and Mass Communication Quarterly*, 77(1).

Gile, D. (2004). Translation Research versus Interpreting Research: Kinship, Differences and Prospects for Partnership. In C. Schäffner (ed.), *Translation Research and Interpreting Research: Traditions, Gaps and Synergies* (pp. 10–34). Clevedon: Multilingual Matters.

Goldscheider, E. (2004). Found in Translation. *Boston Globe Magazine*, 24, 34–42.

Gunter, B. (2003). *News and the Net*. Mahwah, NJ: L. Erlbaum.

Gutiérrez, M. (2006). 'Journalism and the Language Divide'. Paper presented at the Translation in Global News Conference, University of Warwick.

Habermas, J. (1984). What is Universal Pragmatics? In J. Habermas (ed.), *Communication and the Evolution of Society*. Cambridge: Polity.

Hamelink, C. J. (1997). International Communication: Global Market and Morality. In A. Mohammadi (ed.), *International Communication and Globalization*. London: Sage.

Hannerz, U. (1996). *Transnational Connections*. London and New York: Routledge.

——(2004). *Foreign News*. Chicago: University of Chicago Press.

Harper, C. (1998). *And That's the Way it Will Be: News and Information in a Digital World*. New York: New York University Press.

Harvey, D. (1989). *The Condition of Postmodernity*. Oxford: Blackwell.

——(2000). *Spaces of Hope*. Edinburgh: Edinburgh University Press.

Hatim, B. and Mason, I. (1997) *The Translator as Communicator*, London and New York: Routledge.

Headrick, D. R. (1981). *The Tools of Empire: Technology and European Imperialism in the Nineteenth Century*. New York and Oxford: Oxford University Press.

Held, D., McGrew, A., Goldblatt, D. and Perraton, J. (1999). *Global Transformations: Politics, Economics and Culture*. Cambridge: Polity Press.

Herman, E. S. and McChesney, R. W. (1997). *The Global Media: The New Missionaries of Corporate Capitalism*. London and New York: Continuum.

Hernández Guerrero, M. J. (2005a). La traducción de los géneros periodísticos. In C. Cortés Zaborras and M. J. Hernández Guerrero (eds), *La traducción periodística* (pp. 89–133). Cuenca: Ediciones de la Universidad de Castilla-La Mancha.

——(2005b). Prensa y traducción. In C. Cortés Zaborras and M. J. Hernández Guerrero (eds), *La traducción periodística* (pp. 155–73). Cuenca: Ediciones de la Universidad de Castilla-La Mancha.

Holmes, J. S. (1988). *Translated! Papers on Literary Translation and Translation Studies*. Amsterdam: Rodopi.

Hugill, P. J. (1999). *Global Communications Since 1844: Geopolitics and Technology*. Baltimore: Johns Hopkins University Press.

Hursti, K. (2001). An Insider's View on Transformation and Transfer in International News Communication: An English–Finnish Perspective. *Helsinki English Studies*, 1.

Huteau, J. and Ullmann, B. (1992). *AFP: une histoire de l'Agence France-presse: 1944–1990*. Paris: R. Laffont.

IPS. *IPS Style Manual*. Rome.

Jameson, F. and Miyoshi, M. (eds). (1998). *The Cultures of Globalization*. Durham: Duke University Press.

Janelle, D. G. (1991). Global Interdependence and its Consequences. In S. D. Brunn and T. R. Leinbach (eds), *Collapsing Space and Time: Geographic Aspects of Communications and Information*. London: HarperCollins.

Kawamoto, K. (2003). *Digital Journalism: Emerging Media and the Changing Horizons of Journalism*. Lanham: Rowman and Littlefield.

Lash, S. and Urry, J. (1994). *Economies of Signs and Space*. London: Sage.

Lecercle, J. J. (1990). *The Violence of Language*. London and New York: Routledge.

Lefebure, A. (1992). *Havas: les arcanes du pouvoir*. Paris: B. Grasset.

Lefevere, A. (1992). *Translation, Rewriting and the Manipulation of Literary Fame*. London and New York: Routledge.

McLuhan, M. (1964). *Understanding Media: The Extensions of Man*. Harmondsworth: Penguin.

McPhail, T. L. (2006). *Global Communication: Theories, Stakeholders, and Trends* (second edition). Oxford: Blackwell.

Marchetti, D. (2002). L'internationale des images. *Actes de la Recherche en Sciences Sociales*, 145, 71–83.

Marx, K. (1976) *Capital*. London: Penguin.

Mason, I. (1994). Discourse, Ideology and Translation. In R. Beaugrande, A. Shunnaq and M. Helmy Heliel (eds), *Language, Discourse and Translation in the West and the Middle East*. Amsterdam and Philadelphia: Benjamins.

Matterlart, A. (2002). An Archaeology of the Global Era: Constructing a Belief. *Media, Culture and Society*, 24, 591–612.

Miladi, N. (2003). Mapping the Al-Jazeera Phenomenon. In D. K. Thussu and D. Freedman (eds), *War and the Media: Reporting Conflict 24/7*. London: Sage.

Miles, H. (2005). *Al-Jazeera: How Arab TV News Changed the World.* London: Abacus.

Montgomery, M. (1999). Speaking Sincerely: Public Reactions to the Death of Diana. *Language and Literature,* 8, 5–33.

——(2001). Defining 'Authentic Talk'. *Discourse Studies,* 3, 397–405.

——(2005). The Discourse of War after 9/11. *Language and Literature,* 14, 149–80.

——(2006). 'Semantic Asymmetry and "The War on Terror"'. Paper presented at the Translation in Global News Conference, University of Warwick.

——(2007). *The Discourse of Broadcast News: A Linguistic Approach.* London and New York: Routledge.

Muro Benayas, I. (2006). *Globalización de la información y agencias de noticias.* Barcelona: Paidós.

Musa, M. (1997). From Optimism to Reality: An Overview of Third World News Agencies. In P. Golding and P. Harris (eds), *Beyond Cultural Imperialism: Globalization, Communication and the New International Order* (pp. 117–46). London: Sage.

Nickles, D. P. (2003). *Under the Wire: How Telegraphy Changed Diplomacy.* Cambridge, Mass. and London: Harvard University Press.

Niranjana, T. (1992). *Siting Translation: History, Poststructuralism, and the Colonial Context.* Berkeley and Los Angeles: University of California Press.

Orengo, A. (2005). Localising News: Translation and the 'Global–National' Dichotomy. *Language and Intercultural Communication,* 5(2), 168–87.

Palmer, M. (1983). *Des petits journaux aux grandes agences.* Paris: Aubier.

——(1998). What Makes News. In O. Boyd-Barrett and T. Rantanen (eds), *The Globalization of News* (pp. 177–90). London: Sage.

Paterson, C. (1997). Global Television News Services. In A. Sreberny-Mohammadi, D. Winseck, J. McKenna and O. Boyd-Barrett (eds), *Media in Global Context: A Reader* (pp. 145–60). London: Arnold.

——(1998). Global Battlefields. In O. Boyd-Barrett and T. Rantanen (eds), *The Globalization of News* (pp. 79–103). London: Sage.

Paterson, C. and Sreberny, A. (eds) (2004). *International News in the 21st Century.* Eastleigh: University of Luton Press.

Pavlik, J. V. (2001). *Journalism and New Media.* New York: Columbia University Press.

Pym, A. (2004). *The Moving Text: Localization, Translation, and Distribution.* Amsterdam/Philadelphia: John Benjamins.

Rafael, V. (1988). *Contracting Colonialism: Translation and Christian Conversion in Tagalog Society under Early Spanish Rule.* Ithaca: Cornell University Press.

Rantanen, T. (2005). *The Media and Globalization.* London: Sage.

Read, D. (1999). *The Power of News: The History of Reuters* (second edition). Oxford: Oxford University Press.

Reiss, K. (2000). *Translation Criticism: The Potentials and Limitations.* Manchester: St Jerome Publishing, American Bible Society.

Reiss, K. and Vermeer, H. J. (1984). *Grundlegung einer allgemeinen Translationstheorie.* Tübingen: Max Niemeyer.

Reuters. *A Handbook of Reuters Journalism.*

Robertson, R. (1992). *Globalization: Social Theory and Global Culture.* London: Sage.

Said, E. W. (1994). *The Politics of Dispossession.* London: Chatto and Windus.

——(1997). *Covering Islam* (revised edition). London: Vintage Books.

Sapir, E. (1956). *Culture, Language and Personality.* Berkeley: University of California Press.

Sassen, S. (1998). *Globalization and its Discontents.* New York: The New Press.

——(2000). Spatialities and Temporalities of the Global: Elements for a Theorization. *Public Culture,* 12(1), 215–32.

Schäffner, C. (ed.). (2000). *Translation in the Global Village.* Clevedon: Multilingual Matters.

——(2004). Political Discourse Analysis from the Point of View of Translation Studies. *Journal of Language and Politics,* 3(1), 117–50.

——(2005). Bringing a German Voice to English-Speaking Readers: Spiegel International. *Language and Intercultural Communication,* 5(2), 154–67.

Scholte, J. A. (2005). *Globalization: A Critical Introduction* (second edition). Basingstoke: Palgrave Macmillan.

Schudson, M. (1978). *Discovering the News: A Social History of American Newspapers.* New York: Basic Books.

——(1995). *The Power of News.* Cambridge, Mass. and London: Harvard University Press.

Schulte, R. and Biguenet, J. (eds). (1992). *Theories of Translation: An Anthology of Essays from Dryden to Derrida.* Chicago: University of Chicago Press.

Schwartz, V. R. (1998). *Spectacular Realities: Early Mass Culture in Fin-de-Siècle Paris.* Berkeley: University of California Press.

Semprini, A. (2000). *CNN et la mondialisation de l'imaginaire.* Paris: CNRS.

Shaw, M. (2005). *The New Western Way of War.* Cambridge: Polity.

Simeoni, D. (1998). The Pivotal Status of the Translator's Habitus. *Target,* 10(1), 1–39.

Snell-Hornby, M. (2000). Communicating in the Global Village: On Language, Translation and Cultural Identity. In C. Schäffner (ed.), *Translation in the Global Village* (pp. 11–28). Clevedon: Multilingual Matters.

Snell-Hornby, M., Pochhacker, F. and Kaindl, K. (eds). (1994). *Translation Studies: An Interdiscipline.* Amsterdam: John Benjamins.

Sreberny, A. (2002). Collectivity and Connectivity: Diaspora and Mediated Identities. In G. Stald and T. Tufte (eds), *Global Encounters: Media and Cultural Transformation* (pp. 217–33). Luton: University of Luton Press.

Sreberny, A., Winseck, D., McKenna, J. and Boyd-Barrett, O. (eds). (1997). *Media in Global Context: A Reader.* London: Arnold.

Stald, G. and Tufte, T. (2001). *Global Encounters: Media and Cultural Transformations.* Luton: University of Luton Press.

Stetting, K. (1989). Transediting – A New Term for Coping with the Grey Area Between Editing and Translating. In G. Cale (ed.), *Proceedings from the Fourth Nordic Conference for English Studies* (pp. 371–82). Copenhagen: University of Copenhagen.

Thussu, D. K. and Freedman, D. (eds). (2003). *War and the Media: Reporting Conflict 24/7.* London: Sage.

Tomlinson, J. (1999). *Globalization and Culture.* Cambridge: Polity Press.

Tsai, C. (2005). Inside the Television Newsroom: An Insider's View of International News Translation in Taiwan. *Language and Intercultural Communication,* 5(2), 145–53.

——(2006). 'Translation Through Interpreting: A Television Newsroom Model'. Paper presented at the Translation in Global News Conference, University of Warwick.

Tymoczko, M. and Gentzler, E. (eds). (2002). *Translation and Power*. Amherst and Boston: University of Massachusetts Press.

Urry, J. (2000). *Sociology Beyond Societies*. London and New York: Routledge.

Van Ginneken, J. (1998). *Understanding Global News*. London: Sage.

Venuti, L. (ed.). (1992). *Rethinking Translation: Discourse, Subjectivity, Ideology*. London: Routledge.

——(1995). *The Translator's Invisibility: A History of Translation*. London: Routledge.

——(1998). *The Scandals of Translation*. London and New York: Routledge.

Vidal, J. M. (2005). Algunas vivencias de un traductor de prensa. In C. Cortés Zaborras and M. J. Hernández Guerrero (eds), *La traducción periodística* (pp. 379–90). Cuenca: Ediciones de la Universidad de Castilla-La Mancha.

Volkmer, I. (1999). *CNN: News in the Global Sphere*. Luton: University of Luton Press.

Waters, M. (2001). *Globalization* (second edition). London: Routledge.

Wilke, J. (1998). The Struggle for Control of Domestic Markets (2). In O. Boyd-Barrett and T. Rantanen (eds), *The Globalization of News* (pp. 49–60). London: Sage.

Williams, A. (2004). 'Insiders' Views on the Translation of News.' Paper presented at the Translation in Global News Conference, University of Warwick.

Williams, R. (1977). *Marxism and Literature*. Oxford: Oxford University Press.

Index